YOU CAN PAINT YOUR OWN WORLD

POSITIVE BELIEFS THAT LEAD AND GUIDE ME THROUGH LIFE

JERRY SHOWALTER

YOU CAN PAINT YOUR OWN WORLD
by Jerry Showalter

ISBN 13: 978-1-59298-229-5
ISBN 10: 1-59298-229-8

Library of Congress Catalog Number: 2008924734

Book design and page layout: Rick Korab, Punch Design, Inc.
Printed in the United States of America

First Printing: 2009

11 10 09 08 09   5 4 3 2 1

BEAVER'S POND
PRESS

7104 Ohms Lane, Suite 101
Edina, Minnesota 55439 USA
(952) 829-8818
www.BeaversPondPress.com

To order, visit www.BookHouseFulfillment.com or call
1-800-901-3480. Reseller and special sales discounts available

Acknowledgements

I want to recognize my wife, Mary,

for putting up with me as I worked on my book.

Mary was a wonderful support to me as

I wrote the book over a long, slow period of time.

My grandson, Andy, constantly nagged

me to get the job done and finish the book.

If he wasn't an inspiration, at least he was a constant

prod to do what I needed to do.

Thanks Andy!

TABLE OF CONTENTS

Introduction

I have been influenced by many people and many books over my lifetime, and I am thankful for that influence. I have been motivated to action by many different authors. I have had the benefit of going through several Dale Carnegie training courses that have helped me immensely. I have been strongly influenced by the writings of Robert Schuller, Stephen Covey, Zig Ziglar, Norman Vincent Peale, Napoleon Hill, David Schwartz, Jack Canfield, Claude Bristol, Paul Meyers, Albert Lowry, and the list could go on and on. I have some 300 motivational and self-help type books on my living room book shelf that I have read at least once. Some I have probably read up to three times.

I guess what I'm saying is that without that type of influence, my life would have been a lot less fulfilling and productive. I want to thank all 300 of those writers for contributing to my education and my happiness.

My book is somewhat autobiographical and, I hope, a little motivational. There are many different subjects covered about which I have some thoughts and observations that hopefully are useful to some of you. When I read a book, my feeling is that if I can get one idea or thought that I can put to use, then it is a good book. I hope that you will be able to say that you got at least one benefit or idea from this book— matter of fact, I hope that you find many.

—Jerry Showalter

CHAPTER 1

Why Write a Book?

A s I was thinking about writing a book, I had more than one motivating factor to drive me towards actually writing the book. First of all, my three grandchildren are close to me, not only in relationships, but, also, they live close by. But then you ask the question, do they really know that much about me and what makes me tick? And at their age, do they really think about that?

My mother died when grandsons Dane and Andy were around a year and a half old. My dad died in 1968 in Santa Cruz, Bolivia. My point is that my grandchildren have no memory of them because of how young (or nonexistent) they were when their great grand-parents on my side of the family died.

If you sit them down and tell them that they are going to hear the story of the past, the lives of their great grand-parents and how they looked at life, how long would they listen?

But, if it was written in a book, they just might take the time to read the book. Andy had better read it because he has been pushing me for at least a year to get the book written. Andy, this means you have got to read the book because of all the pressure that you have been putting on me to finish the project!

My main purpose in writing the book is to tell my grandchildren what motivated me.

I want to expose them to some of the things that have been and are important to me in my life. I want them to be aware of motivational concepts that are important to me and that hopefully they may find useful in their lives, as they have been to me.

I want them to see and feel some of the ideas that guided my life. I want them to become familiar with some of the outcomes of really believing and living the positive beliefs that lead and guide me in life.

My grandchildren live within a few blocks of us, so you could say that they already know all they need to know or all they want to know about me. Yes, we spend a lot of time together, but do they really understand or believe everything that I'm trying to say? That is not because they are not as smart as I am, because there would be no argument about their being smarter than me. What I want to pass on to my grandchildren are ideas and concepts that have worked for me over the years.

About 9 years ago, when Sami would have been 5 years old and Andy and Dane were 7 years old, I started doing Grandpa Days. I would take one of the grandchildren for a whole day. The reason to take one at a time was that there was always so much competition between the kids for my attention.

This book is not long, so I think the grandkids should be able to stick with it.

CHAPTER 2

My Angel

I saw an angel who appeared to be giving something away. I was curious, so I approached her and asked what she was giving. She said anything that you desire. I said, "Great! I would like success, I want good health, I want lots of friends . . ."

She stopped me and said, "I don't give the fruit, I just give the seed." I told her I didn't understand. She said that she was surprised that I didn't understand that. I told her that I was probably a little slower than most people with whom she talks.

The angel said, "Let me explain this to you. You see, most people think that an angel might give them exactly what they want when they want it. That would be the fruit, but what I give is the seed. The seed is the ideas, tools, and concepts that produce the results that you want, and that is the fruit. The fruit is the end result that you want, like what you asked for, the success, good health, friends, and you'd probably still be talking if I hadn't stopped you."

As I was talking to her, I told her that I planned to write a book and that maybe she could help me do that. I told her that it would help if she gave me some ideas. She said, "Don't you have any ideas of your own?" I said that I could maybe come up with something but that I was hoping for something a little more supernatural, something that might impress my readers a little bit more.

She asked me what I wanted to accomplish with the readers. I told her that I would like to motivate the readers to do something that they might not otherwise do. I want to get them excited about all their possibilities, to develop new dreams, and to make the dreams come true. Give me some ideas to motivate them.

My angel said that she remembered something that she thought was motivational. She said there was this football game that was played on

Thanksgiving Day between the Minnesota Vikings and the Detroit Lions.
I told her that she was talking about a game that took place at least 12 years
ago and that the game was not motivational, because the Vikings had played
a lousy game and lost.

My angel said that it wasn't important who won or lost, but what had been
said during the game. She told me that during the game someone had said
that "on the road of life, there are passengers and there are drivers; drivers
wanted." I said that was a Volkswagen commercial. She said that it didn't
make a bit of difference. Tell your readers to not just be passengers in life and
just go along for the ride wherever someone else is going. Tell them to be
the drivers in life, to be the one who sets a course and makes things happen,
the one who decides what they want to do and to be, to give the direction
to their life.

My angel also said that another thing that was said during that game was
"in life there are those who are going to get around to it — and those who
DO." I said that was the Black and Decker commercial. She said, again that
makes no difference. It's the message. Tell your readers to be ones who
take the initiative, to make positive things happen in life, to avoid being
procrastinators who keep putting off making a difference in their lives.

I told my angel that she had some pretty good ideas to pass on to the
readers, but that I needed something else. She said you really are a little slow.
She said tell your readers to catch a vision. I said that I didn't understand.
She said I guess I will have to tell you a simple story so that even you can
understand, and I'll talk very slowly for you!

She said there was a college professor of music who would tell a story to his
class at the beginning of a new year. He said, "when I was a young boy I took
piano lessons, but I would never practice. I hated to practice. My parents
were constantly yelling at me to practice. They punished me. They rewarded
me. They tried everything to get me to practice, but nothing worked. Then
one day I went to my lesson and there was a new teacher. The teacher said
nothing to me. She just sat down at the piano and played Beethoven's "Moon

light Sonata" and I got excited about what I heard. I caught a vision of what it was like to be an accomplished pianist. When the lesson was over, I was so excited, that I ran all the way home and started practicing. That's why I'm here as a music professor — because I caught the vision."

The angel said, "Tell your readers to catch a vision of what they want to do or be. Tell them to pursue their vision. Tell them to study what they want to do. Tell them to visualize their vision or dream in their mind's eye and work enthusiastically toward their goal."

I asked the angel if she could give me one more idea before she left me. She said why don't you just let me write the book for you. I said no, I really want to do it, but give me one more idea. She said tell them if they are to be successful in what they do that they need to have positive belief. I said explain that to me. She said you're even slower than what I thought you were. I guess I'll have to tell you another story to make sure that you understand what I'm trying to communicate to you.

She told me a story of a tight-wire walker from France named Felipe, who decided he would come to the United States to cross Niagara Falls on a tight wire. The big day for him to do it came. The wire was all set. Felipe started off. Spectators were surprised to see that instead of a long pole to balance himself like most of the people in his trade, Felipe was pushing a wheel barrow with 200 pounds of bricks in it. As Felipe started out things were going just fine until he got to the middle, then the wind started blowing and he was having a tough time staying on the wire. With his great skills he was able to make it over to the other side successfully.

Arriving on the other side, the reporters were interviewing Felipe. Finally, Felipe asked one of the reporters, "Do you think I can make it back?" The reporter said, "Well, you made it over here, so I suppose you could go back too." Felipe said to the reporter, "If you believe that I can, I'll take out the 200 pounds of bricks, and you can get in and we'll go back together." The angel said, "If the reporter gets in, that's POSITIVE BELIEF."

She said tell your readers that if they have a strong positive belief, they can accomplish anything that they set their minds to. They can do anything they want to do or be anything they want to be. She said tell them to use the tools, ideas, and concepts that will be laid out in your book to help produce the results they want in life. Let them know that when we use these tools and ideas, we can change our world, from the inside out.

She said, first of all why don't you include at this point, a talk that I heard you give once. I think the title was "You can paint your own world." I know that you had some of the tools in that talk that turns the seeds into fruit. I said, "I can do that, that will be my next chapter."

NOTES

CHAPTER 3

"You Can Paint Your Own World"

A few years ago Mary and I were in Maui, Hawaii, with some friends. I was standing on the deck of the condo where we were staying. I started looking at all the pretty colors. There was the beautiful blue sky, with white clouds to provide a contrast to the blue sky. Then I looked down at the magnificent blue ocean. I started thinking about how I like to send photo Christmas cards to our friends and relatives, and the fact that I enjoy receiving photo cards from them also.

Then I thought, wouldn't it be great to artificially enhance those already beautiful colors and make the blue of the sky a more brilliant blue? Then bleach out the white clouds so that it would provide even greater contrast? Then I would make the blue ocean sparkle like diamonds.

Later on in the week, I saw something that I'd never seen before. The sky was filled with rainbows, not one or two big ones, but maybe two to three dozen smaller ones. I said to myself YES, I'm going to have a rainbow in my picture too. My friends and relatives are going to say WOW, that Jerry and Mary really go to some beautiful places!

As I was thinking about this, all of a sudden a thought struck me! It struck like a bolt of lightening. That thought was YOU CAN PAINT YOUR OWN WORLD! Each one of us has the ability to do anything that we want to do or be anything that we want to be. We can do it if we can believe that we can. Steve Covey, in his book *The Seven Habits of Highly Effective People* says "to begin with the end in mind." That is one of the seven habits. If we can see with our mind's eye the end result that we want, it will help us to accomplish our goal. If we believe we can, we can. That's a self-fulfilling prophecy. If we believe we can't, we can't. That's also a self-fulfilling prophecy.

Someone may say, that's easy for you to say. "Every time I tell myself I can succeed in what I want to do, something bad happens. I just can't succeed." That's true; bad things do happen to us, but it's not so much what happens to us, but how we react to it. I prefer to replace the word "react" with the word "respond." It sounds like we're in control.

I read a book by Merlyn Carothers, which was titled *Power in Praise*. The theme of this book was when something bad happens to you, thank God for it, because you know that something great will come out of it. I believe it was Napoleon Hill who said "in every adversity there is a seed of an equal or greater benefit." So the message is, when something bad happens, thank God for it and live with great anticipation and wonder about what is about to happen positively. Live in expectancy. It could be beyond our biggest dreams. Remember, our self-fulfilling prophecy. If we think we can, we can; if we think we can't, we can't.

It was in August 1989. It was a Friday. I had just come home to get ready to go to the lake for the weekend. As I walked in the door, the phone was ringing. I answered the phone. One of our employees was reporting that one of our gasoline stations was on fire. She told me that she didn't know how bad it was or if anyone was hurt because the police wouldn't let her get close.

I got into my car and rushed over to the fire. By this time it was under control. The bad news was that the shop and all the equipment was destroyed, as was the roof and roof support system. The electrical wires and box were all burned off. The good news was that no one was hurt, the convenience store was only smoke damaged, and the pumps were intact. This was Friday, and by Tuesday we were pumping gas.

Around a month later, I walk in to the shop. It's all done with bright shiny new construction. Where previously I had probably five-year-old equipment, it was all brand new. Thanks to my insurance company! Now I don't recommend getting new equipment that way, but it was the good that came out of what appeared very bad.

So if each one of us is going to "paint our own world" we each need to become a PAINTER. PAINTER is an acronym as follows:
Passion
Action
Intention
Needs
Thankfulness
Empathy
Resources

First of all we need to have PASSION for what we want to accomplish. We have to be excited about it. We need to feel driven to reach our goals. What's an antonym for passion? Well, probably the word "apathy." There's a condition that's almost as dangerous as apathy, and I would submit that the condition would be complacency. How many of us have had great goals that we want to accomplish? We're well on our way to achieve them, then all the sudden we become pretty comfortable with where we are, and we never give that last effort that it would take to reach our stated goal. Yes, we may be comfortable, but we never did what we really set out to do.

I was at White Bear Lake Rotary Club one morning to give a talk. One of the members, a young dentist, was giving a five-minute classification talk in which he would bring his fellow members up-to-date on what he had been doing. Three or four times in his talk, he used the word passion. He was passionate about what he was doing for his patients. He was using some Scandinavian technology about which he was passionate. Now none of us really like to go to a dentist, but we have to do it, so wouldn't you like to go to a dentist who is passionate about what he or she is doing? Or is that a bad example?

Then we have to take ACTION. Passion without action is not productive. Yes, we have to take action, but we need to have a plan, We need to have INTENTION, which means we have to set goals. So, we do what we have to after we have set the goals. Taking action means taking steps toward your goal.

So we have to know what our INTENTION is. In other words, we have to set our goals. Someone said "success is goals, all else is commentary." That may be a little strong but there is a lot of truth to it. We need to set SMART goals. It helps us to have a formula to make sure that when we set our goals we meet all the requirements of a sound, effective goal. It is also an easy way to remember the steps that we have to take to have a goal that works.

Specific
Measurable
Achievable
Relevant
Time-table for its accomplishment

SPECIFIC We need to specify and quantify exactly what we want to achieve. Increasing sales by $100,000 is very specific. Increasing sales by 10% is also specific, but not as concrete. It is easier to see in your mind's eye the stack of dollars as opposed to a percentage. The more concrete we can make our goal, the more we can visualize it. If it's a goal that we can hear, touch, smell, and see, and we use these senses when reviewing our goals, then we add impact to our goal-achieving process.

MEASURABLE If it's a goal that we can't measure or quantify, we don't really have a goal, but more of a dream. What is the measure? Dollars or pounds? We need a way to monitor our progress. We need to know along the way whether we are on track time-wise versus our goal, so we need a way of measuring what our goal is.

ACHIEVABLE If we set a goal, we must believe that we can do it. If we set a goal too high, maybe to make someone else happy (like the boss), and believe that we can't make it, we are probably right. We can set very high goals, and if we can truly believe that we can do it, we can. It's that same old self-fulfilling prophecy. If we believe we can, we can. If we believe we can't, we can't.

We're probably not going to reach every single goal we set in exactly the right time frame. But where would we have been if we had not set that aggressive goal. Are we unsuccessful if we failed to reach our very aggressive goal? What have we become in the pursuit of our challenging goal? Are we better pre-pared for the next challenge? I think of Hubert Humphrey, who, I heard, had a goal as a young man to be president of the United States of America. He never made it. Was he unsuccessful? He became vice president and he was nominated to be president, but didn't quite make it. What would he have been if he hadn't had that high goal? Not nearly as much, you can be sure.

I believe it was Robert Schuller who said, "I'd rather attempt to do something great and fail than attempt to do nothing and succeed." If we are not chal-lenged by our goals, we are probably not thinking big enough.

RELEVANT If it's not important to us, then we have no reason to set the goal. The goal has to be meaningful to us or we aren't motivated to accomplish it. Don't let someone else convince you of what they think your goal should be. Goals are very personal. If we can't get excited about our goal that we want to set, then we probably shouldn't set it. If we are going to do some really great goal setting, it has to mean something to us. It has to be relevant. You may hear of well-meaning parents who want their child to be a doctor. They may set a goal for one of their children to be a doctor, even if the child has shown no interest in following that path. Maybe the son or daughter even gets into medical school and says to themselves, what am I doing here? I'm not even interested in being a doctor? The goal is not relevant because it was not their goal, it was a parents' goal. A goal, to be relevant, must be a personal goal. You have to really want to reach your goal.

TIME-TABLE We need to have a specific time for the accomplishment of the goal. Most likely we will need check points along the way to make sure that we finish our goal on time. If we have a goal to increase our sales by $100,000 by year's end and if the sales are usually spread out equally, we know that at six months we should have an increase of $50,000 If we don't have that increase, we know we'd better start motivating. A time check gives us a call to action. If we're not where we need to be, we need to take action. There is an urgency to respond when we know that we are behind. That is why there is so much action in the last two minutes of a football game. It's now or never time. My wife tells me that I should only watch the last two minutes of a football game because that's when all the action is. Why is there so much action in the last two minutes? The team that is behind has decided that they had better get with it now or the game is lost. There is an extreme sense of urgency. Hopefully, we don't wait for the last minute to reach our goals, but the goal does spur us on.

Now I'll tell you a personal "goal setting" story, and you can tell me if it was a SMART goal. When I was 29 years old, I told my wife that we will be "well-off" in five years. Was the goal specific? NO. What is well-off? Was the goal measurable? NO, again, how do we measure it? Was it achievable? Maybe it was, who knows? Was the goal relevant? Absolutely, it was important to me. Was there a time-table for it's accomplishment? Yes, five years. My wife immediately took out her permanent record book and wrote "Jerry says we will be well off in five years." So did we make the goal? Who knows, it wasn't a SMART goal. It wasn't specific or measurable.

How do you make your SMART goals an even more powerful tool?

1. Make sure that your goals are written. Keep them in front of you every day and read them. Post them where you will see them. Put up pictures of your goals. They say a picture is worth a thousand words. Add pictures to your goals. Our mind thinks in pictures and sees the end result. Pictures add power!

2. Make a written contract with yourself. Author Jonathan Robinson, in his book titled *Real Wealth*, suggests having a written contract with yourself to tear up two dollar bills if you fail to reach a goal. Not too many of us want to tear up money, so we have a strong incentive to succeed.

3. Commit yourself to making the goal. I heard someone say that "commitment means you don't have to decide." In other words, if we are really committed to a goal and something would detract us from making the goal, we are so committed to that goal, that there is no decision to make. We already made the decision when we set the goal.

Several years ago, I went to the health club where I work out. My son, Jay, who was around 35 years old at the time, came to the club at about the same time I did, normally I was there at 5 AM, but Jay is never going to be there at that time of the morning to exercise, so this must have been a Saturday afternoon. Jay said "Dad, I don't feel like working out." I told him, "Jay, you don't have to." He said "what do you mean, like hit the sauna, steam room, whirl pool, and shower—the executive workout"? I said, Jay you missed the point, you don't have to feel like it, YOU JUST DO IT!

Next we have to deal with NEEDS. There are two types of needs that we need to address. Zig Ziglar said that all we have to do to be successful in life is to find a need and fill it. In other words, we need to provide goods or services that other people need. This could even be preparing ourselves for a job for which there is heavy demand. Maybe it would be finding a product that people need. It's probably not a very good time to go into the buggy whip business. Demand is probably not too high.

The second type of needs is the real needs that people have, whether it's medical, housing, food, and so on. Perhaps some people don't have the resources to provide for themselves and their family. We have an obligation to be a part of the solution. We need to respond out of love for our neighbors, wherever they are in our world.

I am a member of Rotary International. Some of the goals of Rotary are to promote international understanding, and to provide health care, clean water, and all the basic necessities. Programs and projects are being carried out by the 1,225,000 Rotarians in 166 countries. The year 2005, was the centennial year celebration for Rotary. In 2005 we were planning on being able to say that there is not a case of polio in the world. Rotary is the advocate to make this happen, and we have the Rotarian hands across the world to help make it happen. There were some setbacks in the polio eradication program. The world is not yet polio free, but it will soon be polio free.

Are we really as THANKFUL as we should be for all the blessings that we have been given? I believe that we as Americans are the most blessed people in the whole world and as such have an obligation to share our time and our resources with others. Our THANKFULNESS should spill over into doing good for others.

We need to have EMPATHY for our fellowman. This is not just a matter of feeling sorry for someone because of circumstances and problems that they may have, but to really try to walk in their shoes. We need to try to understand what they are going through, and try to help.

Imagine that you're driving on a narrow highway, one lane each way. All of the sudden a car driving about ninety miles an hour is trying to pass you. He lays on the horn, passing you just in time to avoid hitting another car coming from the other way. What are you thinking? What gesture might you be thinking about using? Do you feel a little "road rage"? A lot? Now it's an hour later and you find out that the reason the man was going so fast was that his small son had been injured. It was a life and death race to the hospital. Now how do you feel about it? You're probably saying you'd do the same thing. You feel differently because you now understand the situation. You're walking in the other person's shoes.

Now just imagine that we apply this story to our everyday life. You walk into work one morning. You no sooner sit down at your desk, or what ever you would normally do. A co-worker immediately says something to put you down—not very nice. Your normal reaction would be to respond in kind. Give them a little of their own medicine. But now you remember the speeding car story and you realize that this person probably has a problem. You say to yourself that something probably went wrong at home, maybe an argument with the spouse or the kids. Maybe it's a financial problem or whatever. So, you say to yourself, I've been there, I understand. Your attitude turns from a state of revenge to one of how can I help? Just imagine how low the stress level in your work place would be if everyone would be on that same wave length. We can't control the others, but we can control ourselves. Let's not be a victim of other people's state of mind.

Another thing we need to do is to share our RESOURCES. Our resources are our time, talent, and money. We need to share whatever we have with people who need us or the resources we bring to the table. It's not just what we do for others, but what the doing of it does for ourselves. The Bible says "give and it will be given unto you, good measure, pressed down, shaken together and running over will be put into your lap; for the measure you use to give will be the measure you get back."

Giving is a way of life. Giving is living, and living is giving. So lets be givers and happiness will be with us. Out of an attitude of gratitude, we give because we know we have been blessed. We share and are happy to do it.

Lets each of us commit our self to be a painter and
PAINT OUR OWN WORLD with:

> **Passion**
> **Action**
> **Intention**
> **Needs**
> **Thankfulness**
> **Empathy**
> **Resources**

CHAPTER 4

The Early Years

Before I get involved in talking about all the seeds (tools) that produce the fruit (results), I feel that I need to give a short version of my story. I believe that it will be easier to understand where I am coming from.

My early years up to age seven were lived in Moscow Idaho, which was the home of the University of Idaho. The University was only about a block from my house. I thought that I was a cowboy and dressed that way. I had an adventurous environment, with a lot of freedom and time to explore. I spent a lot of time wandering around the campus. My brother Jim is three years older than I am, and there were, of course, my mom and dad, Elvera, and John. Things would change in our family.

My dad was sitting at the kitchen table on Easter morning in 1941 and for no apparent reason went blind instantly. My dad had come from a family that lived in the Moscow Mountains of Idaho, and church was not a part of their lives. Matter of fact, you could probably count on one hand the number of times that my father had darkened the door of a church (although I don't know that for a fact). My grandfather (paternal) was reported to have been a moon-shiner during the alcohol prohibition era. The home environment in which my dad grew up left a lot to be desired. That blindness was a touch from God to get my dad's attention.

During the period that dad was recovering and his sight came back, my dad listened to a religious program called "The Light of the World." As a result of listening to that program, and some counseling from his brother-in-law, my dad had a spiritual awakening, and gave his life to the Lord. That was a new beginning for my dad and the rest of the family. It set a new path in front of our whole family. My dad's eyesight recovered nearly one hundred per cent over time.

After recuperating from his blindness, my dad returned to his work at the lumber yard in Moscow, Idaho, where he was the bookkeeper, along with some other responsibilities. When he got back to work, he was restless and felt like he should be doing something else. He had no idea what that "something else" was. He resigned and took a job as a carpenter at the Naval training base at Lake Pend Oreille in Idaho.

This was war time. He only worked there around six months as he was feeling like he should be doing something else. He didn't know what. He quit his job without knowing what he was going to do next. It was a step of faith that God would lead him to what he should be doing

The following Monday he went to the pastor's house to return a book that dad had borrowed from him. The pastor had no idea that he had quit his job, but after greeting him, the first thing the pastor said was, "How would you like to go to Bolivia?" What he meant was to go to Bolivia as a missionary. Dad knew that this was the calling that he was waiting for. But was he prepared? Not at all. He had no theological training whatsoever. He was a brand-new Christian with a calling, but no training to do what he was being called to do. He had little financial resources (like nothing!) and a family to support. But God was calling and he was ready to answer that call. I don't think that up to this point that he had ever attempted to do any public speaking, but there was this call.

Soon, Dad was enrolled at the Lutheran Bible Institute in Minneapolis. Mom, my brother Jim, and I were left behind in Moscow, Idaho. Mom got a job in a bakery to earn some money. She had never worked outside the home before. I don't know exactly how we survived financially. During the summers, Dad worked in the grain harvest filling and tying sacks of grain as he rode on the combine. This was in the Colfax, Washington, area.

After two years, our family headed to Minneapolis in our Model A Ford. In this era you felt that having only two or three flat tires along the way was a successful trip. This was the year of 1944. Dad would finish his studies at the Lutheran Bible Institute in 1945. He would not be considered a pastor in the United States, but he would be when he got to Bolivia.

My dad and mom were accepted and commissioned to go to Bolivia by The World Mission Prayer League headquartered in Minneapolis. The WMPL is a Lutheran missionary organization, but not a part of any particular Lutheran synod. It is called a faith mission. My definition of a faith mission is that if enough money comes in to the mission, you get paid a very small salary, and if it doesn't come in, then you may get some or none. You have to have a LOT of faith.

We found out very early in the game the value of prayer and faith. When we left for Bolivia in August of 1945, I was 10 years old and my brother Jim was 13. We left by train to go to New Orleans to get on an Argentine ship that would take us to Callao, Peru. There was only one problem. We still didn't have enough money to pay for the passage we had booked on the ship. The money was wired to us just an hour or two before the ship was to leave. We had just enough money to get to Peru, and we still needed to take a Chilean ship to Chile and a train from Chile, at sea level, to the 10,000 feet altitude of La Paz. God is faithful and when we got to Peru, money was wired to us there to complete the trip. A good start for us to know that God would supply.

While we were on the Chilean ship (which by the way, was like a fishing bobber or cork that made you seasick even when you were in the harbor) one of the ship's stewards who spoke no English, and of course we spoke no Spanish, came to give us this message: "bang, bang, finished." He was telling us that the Second World War was over. Good news! We arrived at Arica, Chile, where we stayed for a night before making our journey by train to our destination of La Paz, Bolivia.

It wasn't a particularly easy transition to get started in Bolivian life because of the high altitude and the language barrier. After a couple weeks, the altitude is conquered. The Spanish takes a little longer. Mom and Dad had to study the language, but Jim and I picked it up on the street quickly. When I say that Jim and I picked up the language on the street, it is pretty true, as we played soccer in the street with the Bolivian kids using nylon stockings stuffed with rags for the soccer ball.

Early on, Jim and I were looking across the street at a store that sold candy, which we thought looked pretty good. We wondered how to ask the price, not that we would have understood the response! We decided that since in Spanish the word *como* was how, and that *mucho* was much, that we could say *como mucho* or how much. Fortunately we didn't try at that point, as what we would have been saying is "I eat a lot." *Comer* means to eat, and the conjugation of the verb to say I eat, is *como*.

Jim and I had a lot of freedom to explore, we walked all over the large city of La Paz. We experienced revolutions. There were something like three or four revolutions while we were there for our four years. In the revolution we would hoist the American flag at our house, which gave us some protection. One of these revolutions was so intense that you wonder, if this is a revolution, what would a war be like? As the revolution waned, the soldiers were still patrolling the streets around the presidential palace. Jim and I were asking for (and receiving) live bullets for our souvenirs. Jim and I have never been known for our great judgment!

NOTES

CHAPTER 5

Adventure

In Bolivia, my brother, Jim, and I didn't go to the local schools. Mrs. Duncan a missionary, who came to Bolivia about the same time as we did, was our teacher. She had a very small school, only 3 to 6 kids as I recall. The school started in the city of La Paz. After the first year it was moved to the mission farm named Coaba. Coaba was a very large farm that served as a headquarters for the area mission work. I don't know how many acres it was, but it had its own small mountain range and three rivers that flowed (flowed may not be the best choice of words, as at times it cascaded over a series of water falls) through and at it's borders. Aside from the tillable land, it was very rugged. The farm also provided jobs for the local Bolivian Indians (the poorest and lowest class). These Indians lived in a very small village of Cheje within a mile of the Coaba farm. At that time the Indians accounted for about 90 percent of the population of the country. There was a small middle class and an even smaller first class.

Coaba not only provided the much-needed jobs for the Indians, but it also gave us a base of people to evangelize. On the farm, we had a thatched-roof, open-air church. The main language of these local people was Aymara, which is a very hard language to learn. One of the reasons it's so hard to learn is there are so many guttural sounds.

The farm gave Jim and me many places to explore: the rugged mountains, the rivers, the water-falls, and oh yes, the caves. If Mom and Dad had known what we were doing, they probably wouldn't have slept nights. Exploring the caves was pretty scary, but stupidity knows no fear, and we qualified in that department pretty well.

We also had an all-night search for two of our missionary's daughters, who had evidently lost their way. We had teams out looking for them. Jim and I were together. We were going in places by the rivers that we weren't sure we could get back up if we went down, or if we could get down without slipping on the wet boulders. The waters of the rivers were swift and the water falls treacherously high and dangerous. In the dark, we didn't always know what we were getting into. If our parents would have known what we were doing, they would have panicked.

Fortunately the two girls were found. They ended up on a rocky shelf, where they decided they had better stay for the night. The next morning a native from a nearby village found them and helped them get out of their predicament.

NOTES

CHAPTER 6

Dad

M y dad's favorite thing to do in Bolivia was to travel the mule trails to other towns, where he would have a chance to preach the gospel. In some cases the trips were fairly extensive, taking days. I believe, among other things, he enjoyed the freedom of being alone on the trails. Mules are the best way to "fly" on the rocky, steep, narrow, and treacherous trails. Horses are not as sure footed as the mules and donkeys, and believe me "sure footed" is very important on these trails. The trails are uneven, and a fall by the mule and rider could send them over the edge to some kind of unhappy ending.

The altitude is also a big issue on cross country travel, especially if one is walking. I remember trying to catch my mule on one of these trips across the "altiplano" or, in English, the high plains. The elevation was something like twelve to fourteen thousand feet above sea level, and by the time I caught her, I was really exhausted. You learn to remain in charge and in control of your mule. At least on the high flat plains you're not going to fall over the edge of the trail!

My dad liked to camp out when we crossed the altiplano. One time when we camped out in the altiplano, Dad was concerned about me because my heart was pounding so hard that he could hear it during the night. Elevation has great impact. Dad liked to hunt, and in the area where we camped he would hunt viscachas, which were something similar to squirrels. It felt good to come down the other side of the mountain after crossing the high plains. We would then get down to the low altitude of only seven or eight thousand feet.

Dad would travel a lot alone. On one of these trips, he was traveling from our home town of Mocomoco to a town called Charizani, which I suppose was about 25 miles away. The only way to get there was by mule. He had started from home at seven thousand feet above sea level. He would travel at between twelve and fourteen thousand feet until he reached the summit at about fifteen thousand. This is a completely uninhabited area and potentially

dangerous. As Dad arrived at the summit, he looked around and saw no one. He started his descent and immediately a man on horse or mule appeared out of nowhere. He had on a poncho, which seemed to be hiding a bulky gun across his lower back. The man asked for some drugs, I think coca. Was this a diversion? Dad pulled out his New Testament Bible and said, "I don't use coca; I use the Word of God!" The man disappeared quickly and caused Dad no harm. God was with Dad and kept him safe.

Another time my mom and dad were traveling together by mule. Many of the rivers did not have bridges, so one would have to cross the river by mule. This day the river water was exceptionally swift and high and, of course, the river is rocky. All of these factors make it a very hazardous crossing. As they were carefully trying to cross the river, Mom's horse fell and she was in the water. My dad was almost giving up on trying to save her, when he knew he had to make a valiant effort to save her. He went into the water, and he said that it was if there was no current. He was able to save her. Again God showed his power and concern.

Dad liked some of the native foods that the rest of the family didn't care for at all. He would cook two local foods in the pressure cooker, and when the pressure released, what a smell! Obviously, this is not the way the Bolivians cooked theirs! If my memory serves me right the two foods were called "tuntas" and "chunos." The tuntas, as I recall, were some sort of dried potato type food, and the chuno was dried sheep meat. I guess he was a little more adventurous than the rest of the family.

CHAPTER 7

Missionary Work

My mom and dad, of course, had their own missionary work to do. They were first assigned to work in La Paz, a city of around a million people. The city looks like it's in a bowl, with hills or mountains going up on the sides. Snow-capped mountains are a beautiful sight from La Paz. The altitude of La Paz is around ten thousand feet.

My parent's next assignment to do their mission work was a small town of Mocomoco, which may have had a population of around two thousand people. All the houses were constructed in one way or another from mud with straw mixed in to hold it together and either straw or tile for the roofs. Many of the floors were only packed dirt.

Mocomoco was about 90 miles away from La Paz. This sounds close, but with the road conditions as they were, it would take a whole day to get there. They were dirt roads with many bumps. We would travel on top of all the cargo that would be stacked up to the top of the side racks of the trucks. We would leave La Paz at ten thousand feet of altitude and ascend to the "altiplano" at an altitude of some twelve thousand feet. We would travel most of the way at that elevation. We might come close to Lake Titicaca along the way. Then we would start descending to Mocomoco, which would be at about 7,000 feet of altitude. The slow descent is very mountainous and has hair pin curves. On the worst ones a helper will place a block in front of or in back of a wheel as the truck driver maneuvers the truck around the turn. He will start around the curve, back up, block, go ahead, block, until he gets around the turn. You can understand why it can take so long.

CHAPTER 8

School Days

J im and I were away from Mom and Dad for most of the time for the two years that our missionary kid's school was at the Coaba farm and they were stationed in Mocomoco. The last year we were in Bolivia, we didn't have a missionary kid's school as Mrs. Duncan had returned to the U.S. We were then planning on doing our last school year in Bolivia by the Calvert correspondence course that we would do at home in Mocomoco. Money came in to pay for the course, we thought. It turned out that the money would be used to get us through six months in which no salary money was available from the World Mission Prayer League. But the Lord supplied. As a result of studying at home without an approved course (not only not approved, but almost non-existent), Jim didn't get any credit for the year, so he came into high school as a sophomore, instead of a junior. They let me get credit for the year, as mine was the eighth grade that I missed, and I started in high school as a freshman.

When we knew that we were returning for the 1949 school year, Jim and I started looking at where we wanted to go to school. It had to be a boarding school because during the year my parents would be home. They would be touring churches to tell their story and to raise money to keep going. Then after the one-year home, they would return to Bolivia for three to four years for the next term. So for the next four years we were "stored" at Augustana Academy in Canton, South Dakota (about twenty-four miles from Sioux Falls). I say "stored" rather facetiously as I enjoyed the school. In a church school, every thing you do is wrong, so consequently every thing is fun. I received the penalty of doing twenty-one work hours (cleaning the hallways in the men's dormitory) for "getting caught" going with some friends to the show "THE MOON IS BLUE." Movies were off limits. It doesn't take much to stir up some excitement. How many kids have three years when they don't have to answer to their parents? I wasn't really the rebel that I make it sound like. I played sports, had good friends, and had a good time.

CHAPTER 9

Summer Time

D uring the summers, Jim and I would go out West, by one means or another, to work in the green pea and grain harvests in Oregon, Washington, and Idaho. We would start out in green peas and finish in wheat, then we'd head back to school and football practice. We had relatives in Idaho to spend some time with if times were slow.

During the green pea harvest we had all kinds of different jobs and responsibilities. We started out by pitching the peas on their vines with a pitchfork into the stationary viner, which shelled the peas out. The peas ended up in the hoppers on the sides. It was a four-person job to keep a pair of viners going. Two of us would be pitching in the pea vines (which was heavy work), while the other two would be emptying the hoppers of peas into boxes and would get a chance to rest up a little before the next round of pitching the pea vines.

We talked one of the farm owners into letting three of us, Jim, my cousin Larry, and me, do the work of four people and getting the pay of the phantom fourth person divided up between the three of us. These were twelve-hour days so it was long, hard work. Many times I would start out in the morning when my wrists were so sore that picking up a cup of coffee hurt my wrists. You then start pitching the pea vines and forget about those little pains.

Over the years of working in the peas, we ended up doing a lot of other duties, like driving trucks, swathing the peas, and getting the pea vines loaded into the trucks.

After finishing the pea season, it would be time to start working in the wheat harvests. Jim would be driving a track-type tractor since a good share of the wheat fields were very steep and a wheel-type tractor couldn't do the job. I would either drive trucks or "punch header" on the wheat combine.

Punching header meant that I was controlling the blade that was cutting the wheat at the right level and I was also keeping the combine level. This was important as some of the fields were almost mountainous. As we would come to a downhill corner, I would have to anticipate when to start compensating for the steep incline, so that we wouldn't tip over.

CHAPTER 10

COLLEGE

B rother Jim decided to attend Waldorf College in Forest City, Iowa. He was a year ahead of me in school. When I graduated from Augustana Academy, I decided to attend there also. Waldorf was a very small college then. Waldorf was a junior college, so I could go there just two years. The two years I played football there, I played both offense and defense, not because I was so good but because of the limited number of football players. In the two years I played football, I was only out of the football games for 30 seconds, that being in the last 30 seconds of the last game of my last year. The last time I attended a game there, the guys were big enough to be pro players, and they also had the numbers of players. Just goes to show, like everything else in life, timing is everything.

I had a small scholarship to play football at Augustana College in Sioux Falls after I graduated from Waldorf. I was at Augustana College only about three or four weeks when I decided to call it quits for several reasons. One of the big ones was I had no money. I decided to go to work. It only took me about a month to decide I didn't want to be in the insurance business. I had gone to work for a company that sold hospitalization insurance. I would drive through the farm country of Iowa and stop at every farm in the area to which I was assigned for the day. It wasn't my idea of a fun job, and I was gone quickly.

CHAPTER 11

My Career

I went to work for the Standard Oil Company. Six months in the mail department, six months shipping supplies from the stationary department, then a year as mail department supervisor, two years in accounting, one year in the marketing department, then five years supervising service station operators, and my final five years as territory manager supervising bulk agents who delivered petroleum products and agricultural products to farm, residential, and commercial customers.

About two years before I left Standard Oil Company I took a Dale Carnegie Training Sales class for ten weeks. This class absolutely changed my life. I can't name one thing that made all the difference. It was in several areas of my life. When I left that class, I had more confidence, I was more comfortable speaking to groups of people, I was a more positive person who understood the value of goal setting. I realized that I got out of myself what I fed myself, mentally and positively. I realized that there is power in goal setting, that when you write it down, work, and believe that you can accomplish it, great things happen. I was not the same person, and I looked for opportunities to make my world bigger.

I decided that I wanted to go into business for myself, so I started looking for those opportunities. I decided that I wanted to be in control of what happened. In large corporations decisions are made, and everyone makes commitments to employees and other stakeholders based on those decisions, only to find that the commitments you made can get changed because of a new manager in the chain of command. That person decides they have a better answer. In that case the decision that I made is overruled. If I make a commitment, I want to keep it. It helps to be your own boss to be able to keep the commitments you make.

As I was looking for business opportunities, one thing I didn't want to do was to lease a full-service gasoline service station. The reason I say that is because most of the people who operated service stations, at that time, were mechanics or mechanically inclined. Not me! But then I noticed that there was a new Standard Oil Company service station being built in Roseville, Minnesota, a suburb of St. Paul. I felt that this would be a good location, so I made the decision to put in my application for it.

At times there was a policy not to let someone who was a company employee leave and take over a station. The time was right, and I was given the opportunity to have a business of my own. You always have a few doubts about whether one is doing the right thing. Going on your own in business is a big step. As the station was being finished, it appeared as though the county might not give us access from our most important street. I was concerned about this possibility. I talked about this possibility with my wife, Mary, about how she felt about going ahead with this business in view of the fact that there could be some negatives due to the possible limited access. She was positive about the situation, so we went ahead. The negative never developed in all the time we owned the station. It's great to have a wife who gives this kind of support so that you know it's a joint decision.

NOTES

CHAPTER 12

A New Business

I was an employee of Standard Oil Company for nearly 15 years, from 1955 to July 31, 1970, and the next day, August 1, I was in business for myself. I had about $3,000 for operating capital and a loan for stock and equipment from Standard Oil (that has not been available for many years). Timing is everything.

At that time, a Standard Oil dealer could lease only one station, unless, of course, the company had a location that they couldn't find someone to operate. Then they might consider letting a dealer have two locations. Then in approximately 1976, the state passed some new franchise laws that made our leased operations become franchises in the legal sense, and with that came some new rights and protection. One of the big changes made it possible to buy a service station business directly from another service station dealer without having the company involved in the transaction. The business itself now had value beyond the value of inventory and equipment. Now there was also the "Good Will" value of business. I was the first Standard Oil dealer to take advantage of the new Minnesota laws.

With the franchise law change, I was now able to expand over time to 5 Standard Oil (Amoco BP) stations. (Timing is everything!) When this was happening, I realized the value of not being a mechanic if you want to expand your business. It's hard to grow other businesses if you have your head under the hood. At one point I had six service stations, three muffler shops, an auto parts store, and several real estate rental properties. By the way, not everything always turns out the way you think it should. The bad news is that the muffler shops didn't work out for me. The good news is that the real estate that went with the shops worked out fine.

Real Estate Investments

 nd now, going back in time and talking about real estate, in about May or June of 1977, a casual acquaintance asked me if I would go with him to a real estate seminar that would take place over a weekend in downtown Minneapolis. This was one of those no-money-down, low-money-down type seminars for buying commercial property. After taking the course, I decided that it was something that I wanted to do and could do. By September I was able to buy a small office building in the Minneapolis suburb of New Hope. In November I bought a very small four-unit strip commercial building.

Setting goals had become a way of life to me. In December 1977, I set my goals for the year 1978. One of those goals was in acquiring real estate. I set what for me was a big goal at the time. The goal was to add $750,000 of real estate for 1978. I didn't have too much cash, but I refinanced our house and with a little other money added, I now had $70,000 for down payments with which to buy real estate.

In December, I started looking in the want ads to start working on the 1978 goal. I ran across an ad for a forty-unit townhouse complex complete with swimming pool. I called the realtor to get the details. He said that the price was $1,100,000 with $250,000 down and they would carry a contract for deed at 8% interest for 15 years. If you could get those kinds of prices today that would be great, but times were very different. I told the realtor that this was too much for me and forgot about it until January. Remember, I only had $70,000 for a down payment.

In January 1978, I was looking at the want ads and saw the same ad. I called the realtor and told him that we had to get together to talk about it, that there must be some way we could work it out. We got together and I offered $1,000,000 with $70,000 down (that's all I had) and an 8% contract for 15 years. The realtor took the offer to the owner, who refused it. The owner didn't really make a counter offer, but said that he needed $1,100,000.

So now it's time to make another offer. I figured that maybe the most important issue to him was the $1,100,000, but maybe I could negotiate a better interest rate. I then offered $1,100,000 (full price) with my $70,000 down payment (did I say that's all I have?) and a 15-year contract at 7% for the first 10 years and 8% for the last 5 years. The one percent interest savings in this offer would just a little more than offset the extra $100,000 that I would pay by giving the asking price.

Although the deal had not closed, I started acting mentally as though I already owned it. I started thinking and acting as though the deal had closed, and I was making the changes necessary to do what I wanted and needed to do. I was working out deals mentally that would make it a more profitable investment. I started looking at how I could increase profits by changing who was paying some of the expenses, like water, which at that time was not metered. By looking at these opportunities, it was like I already owned the buildings. This was a positive step. I was, in fact, already acting as though I had control over what was happening in my new investment. Positive belief makes great things happen!

One thing that really helped me in dealing with the owner was that I was able to meet with him and his wife in person along with the real estate sales person, compared to always working through the realtor only as the mouthpiece. When I found that I was getting the opportunity to interact with the owners personally, I prepared for the occasion.

I put together a notebook type of presentation. I had included pictures of my house, my two investment properties that I had at the time, and my two gasoline service stations. I had profit and loss statements on each of the stations that were prepared by my accountant included in the presentation booklet. The impact of this presentation on the owner and his wife was very obvious. The wife said to her husband, "why don't we do something like that?" She was impressed, and it helped to move us along in the buying process.

The owner finally verbally committed to sell the complex to me, but obviously verbal doesn't mean much; you need the signature. I had a goal, $750,000 and here it was within my grasp and then some. Mentally, I claimed the complex as mine. I owned it mentally. I acted as if I already really owned it. I worked out ways to decrease expenses or increase revenue. Yes, I didn't really own it until we got the signed agreement and closed on it, but mentally it was already mine. Now it was a fact. It was mine. We closed the deal successfully.

When a person gets involved in something bigger than what we're used to, it's too easy to get cold feet and say this is too big, what am I doing? I had some of those thoughts. I thought is this too big for me? Am I getting in over my head? Then I remembered my goal of $750,000 and thought, wow! not only do I achieve my goal, but exceed it by $350,000 in one transaction. Goals give us courage and keep us on target. Goals give us a sense of urgency and confidence. Goals mean that we are committed to the task. If we are really committed to the goal and we have an open door to complete it, we need to go for it.

Before leaving real estate concepts completely, I want to say one thing I did aggressively for many years, which I felt was advantageous to me, and if not to me at least to the realtor. If I decided that I really didn't care for the property or the price, I would make a low offer anyway. My feeling was if I get it at this price, it's a good deal. If they aren't interested in what I offer, the realtor has something to talk about with his or her client. Maybe it would help the client and/or the realtor to determine what is a fair price so they can make sure they are realistic in their asking and selling price.

Mary and I were out to eat with another couple that are our friends. Jack and I had worked together as sales people at Standard Oil. Jack mentioned that a person he knew was buying rental homes in Phoenix, Arizona. Jack said this acquaintance thought that it was a good time to buy as prices were undervalued. Also, although interest rates were high (1981–82), around 15 percent (Jimmy Carter times), we could assume lower cost mortgages and have the seller carry a contract for deed after a small down payment. I told

Jack to get out his calendar so that we could set up a time when we and our wives could go to Phoenix to look at this opportunity. We set the date to go to Phoenix that night. Jack agreed to call a realtor to set up a date so we could look for rental houses.

Within about two weeks we all were in Phoenix to look at buying some houses. The realtor had about nine houses set up on appointments for us to look at in one day. We didn't waste much time. We made an offer on at least eight of the houses. At the end of the day we had bought two houses and after some counter offers by the next day we had four. In a short time we ended up with eight rental houses there.

Now this is a great deal, right? The prices for the houses are really right. Our interest rate is averaging around ten and a half percent in a fifteen percent market.

So, everything looks like a big win. Interest rates will never go down, and house prices will go up. Well, the interest rates went back down and the house prices were staying pretty much the same. All of the houses were not rented all the time.

After about a year and a half, my friend, Jack, says let's get out of this. I said, I will buy you out. He was very happy to be out of it. Mary and I held on to the houses for several years. It gave us a good excuse to go to Phoenix, and it was fun. Jack says I'm his best friend for getting him out of it. So everything ended well. Goals kept me on track to pursue what we wanted to accomplish in real estate. (Even if this deal didn't work out the way it is supposed to.)

NOTES

CHAPTER 14

Success

We talk a lot about success. What is success? Success means different things to different people. Success is feeling good about yourself, about what you have become and are becoming. Success is enjoying your work. Success is having a positive outlook on life.

You may say, "I am not successful, I haven't accomplished very much." Maybe your idea of success is entirely different from mine. Each of us is different. Success to one person may be making a lot of money. Success to another may be making a difference in the world. Maybe it is teaching children, or maybe it is helping people who have health needs. We could go on and on. If we're happy in what we're doing and it's productive, we are successful. We don't have to be concerned about what someone else thinks. It's what we think. What's good for someone else, may not be our thing. Let's not let others control our happiness or our sense of self-worth. Each of us is unique. We don't need to compare ourselves to others. It would be a boring world if we all wanted the same thing out of life.

Paul Meyer of Success Motivation Institute in Waco, Texas, gave this definition of success: "Success is the progressive realization of a worthwhile, predetermined personal goal." In other words, you know what you want, (your personal goal) and are constantly working toward that goal. You are always showing personal growth in the process.

Success is a good self-image. Someone said that people act like they think they are. If they feel they are successful, they are. I repeat, success is different things to different people. You act out the way that you feel you are. If you get the results that you expect and work toward, you are successful. Yes, there are people who the world would say are more successful than you or me, but in achieving what you personally want, you are truly successful. You are successful!

Success doesn't necessarily mean to get. It doesn't necessarily mean to have a stack of money. Now that's just fine, but it's not just to get but to become. It's to become the person that you want to be. If in the process of "getting," you become someone who you don't like or don't want to be, you have failed in the "success journey."

You don't measure your success by comparing it to what others have done. You don't measure yourself by what others do or do not accomplish.

We all have different strengths and weaknesses, so we need to strive to be the best that we can be, and not compare our abilities to others, good or bad. If we limit our success by saying or feeling that we are already more successful than he or she is, we are not using our full potential. If on the other hand, we say that another person is so successful that there's no way we can match that person's success, and slack off, we are not reaching our potential.

We can ask many questions about success. To be successful, do we have an obligation to grow? Do we have an obligation to help others? Is success controlling what happens to us, or is it responding successfully to what happens to us? Successful living must be well rounded, but what is success for one isn't necessarily success for another. We all have different abilities and capabilities. Success is doing the best we can with what we have been given.

Successful living involves a positive mental attitude, being goal oriented and involved. Successful living is forgiving others in spite of what they may have done to us. Life is too short to hold grudges. It's not so much what happens to us in life but how we respond to what happens to us that makes a difference in our lives. Even if something bad happens to us or we think that we have been mistreated, we need to respond positively, believing, and knowing that good will come from it. Success is an attitude, a good attitude. Someone said, we live moment by moment, not year by year. Success isn't all of the sudden success is every day.

In a 1978 cartoon of "Kathy" by Cathy Guisewite, Cathy's friend, Andrea, is responding to Cathy's addiction to smoking and the struggle to quit. She says to Kathy, "there's no such thing as permanent success in anything in life. Success only lasts as you repeat the right decisions." Now that's a profound statement, and this was in a cartoon! When we are successful we have to keep on making the right decisions over and over again. We cannot say, "I am successful, so I can slack off and take things easy."

If we want to be a success and we don't feel as though we are successful, what can we do to turn the corner? We can act successful. Acting doesn't necessarily make it so, but it helps us to believe in ourselves. Belief produces results in our lives. We need to act as if we are successful and believe. Believing does great things for us. There is power in believing! We can feel good about what we have accomplished already, and know that we can achieve, because we believe and hustle!

Success is not measured by how you do compared to how somebody else does. Success is measured by how you do compared to what you could have done with what God gave you. (This is from one of those daily calendar pad pages.)

CHAPTER 15

Positive Mental Attitude

A re you dressed for success? I'm not talking about having exactly the right clothes to wear to create a great first impression. What I'm talking about is having the right attitude towards people and the right attitude toward our own opportunities to succeed in every area of our lives.

You may not read anything new in this book about a positive mental attitude, anything that you don't already know. Each of us comes to a time in our life, hopefully, when it makes sense to us, and there's a new understanding. Maybe it's an idea whose time has come in our lives. Maybe today is the day when it all makes sense. Maybe today is the day that we want to make changes in our life. Maybe today we have decided that we want more out of life. As the saying goes, when the student is ready, the teacher will appear. Is today the day? Let's look for new meaning in our lives.

I personally am excited about a positive mental attitude. I would contend that the right attitude changes lives. The reason that I can say that with some authority is that my life was changed, as I mentioned before, by taking a Dale Carnegie sales course. It acquainted me with the value of how important it is to fill our minds with positive belief, a belief that we can achieve almost anything we want. My life was changed, not just by achievement but by the way that I felt about life. I was exposed to new ideas and concepts of which I was not previously aware.

At this point, it was as if everything was new. I was asked to do things that I'd never done before. It was as though I had changed, and people could tell the difference. (That's my opinion!)

I stayed on as a group leader at Dale Carnegie (unpaid assistant-type person) to help during the classes. It was interesting for me to see what people were like when they came into the class and the changes that took place by the time they finished. I saw some who made no changes because they already had all the answers. I saw others who were excited about what they were learning. We all need to keep an open mind as to what we can do to be more successful in every area of our lives. We don't have all the answers, and we don't have to, but we need to concentrate on growth in our lives. It is interesting to me that as I talk to people at all levels, if I mention that I took the Dale Carnegie course and how it changed my life, they will say something like "you too?" Then they will tell their story.

One acquaintance, when I mentioned that I had taken a Dale Carnegie course and that it had changed my life, said "you too?" He proceeded to tell me how he was so afraid to speak in front of groups of people, then took the Dale Carnegie course and was asked to be the king of the Saint Paul Winter Carnival. He gave some 500 talks and enjoyed every minute of it. Another friend told me that he had taken a Dale Carnegie course and had improved so much. He had been promoted to a top position in a large company, like 15,000 employees. He felt that his presence in this company was important and that he was able to communicate with large groups of employees very effectively because of his Dale Carnegie training.

I believe that setting goals is an important part of maintaining a positive mental attitude (PMA). We need to individually take a look at what's standing in the way of what we want to be or do. Then we need to take positive action steps to maintain a PMA and a "successful" life, whatever that means to each of us. It certainly is something different to each of us.

The PMA we're talking about isn't an attitude that says, life is great, I don't have a problem in the world, I can just sit here and enjoy the world as it passes me by. A truly successful life involves many aspects, and the most important is our personal relationship with Jesus Christ. Yes, other things are important, but first things first.

I remember going to an inspirational, motivational rally many years ago in a large Minneapolis auditorium. There were probably 10,000 people there. One thing that really impressed me was that speaker after speaker expressed their positive relationship with Jesus Christ. I couldn't help but wonder how the people who didn't have a spiritual relationship felt about the message and what they were missing. These speakers were Paul Harvey, Zig Zigler, Earl Nightengale, Clement Stone, Norman Vincent Peale, and Robert Schuller. It made me feel that a really positive attitude begins with Jesus Christ.

In my opinion, a positive mental attitude involves constructive action. If we have a positive attitude but do nothing with our lives, then what have we gained? Our positive mental attitude affects every area of our lives. We are not one-dimensional people. We need to be well-rounded individuals. We need to consider our business or vocational life, our social life, our mental development, our physical well-being, and our family life. If we are focused on only one area of our lives only, we are headed for trouble.

How is our vocational life? Do we go to work every day dreading what we have to do, or are we excited about what we are doing? Are we just putting in our hours and thinking only about how glad we'll be when work is over for the day? Are we giving our employers a fair day's work? If we are going to work with a PMA and are really looking forward to what we can do for our company, then we will get rewarded not only in the satisfaction we get out of the job, but we will be rewarded with praise for a job well done, and the spendable compensation that goes with it. PMA pays!

Our social lives are an important part of living. PMA makes our relationships better as we become good company. We are not only concerned about ourselves, but also about our friends. We are not in the relationship just for what we can get out of it, but also for what we can give. Are we spreading positive vibes and goodwill to our friends? Do we let them know that they mean a lot to us? Do we let them know that we appreciate them and tell them so?

Are we satisfied with where we are in our mental development? Are we challenging ourselves to grow mentally, or are we content to just stagnate? Just because we are supposedly adults doesn't mean that we don't need to enhance skills that benefit us in every area of our lives. We know what our weaknesses are. Let's have the attitude that we need to keep on growing.

We as human beings are also spiritual beings, and if we ignore that fact, we miss out on many of the greatest blessings in life. There is something spiritual about a positive mental attitude. When we really believe that we can do something and have faith that we can achieve it, we add a new dimension to our lives. Jesus himself said, "All things are possible to him who believes." Now if that isn't a good example of PMA, I don't know what is, and it comes right from the Source! Spiritual strength is very important to successful living.

How do we take care of the physical side of our lives? Are we committed to keeping ourselves fit? It is so easy to just slide through our days and our weeks without the proper diet and without exercising the way we should. Does it take effort and commitment? Yes, it does. Is it worth the effort and commitment? Yes, it is. We have to make physical fitness a habit. There are good habits and there are bad habits. Fitness is a great habit. Physical fitness affects every other area of our life. We have the energy to do anything that we want to do. Whether it is for the job we're doing or fun, we have the energy and stamina.

Some may think that it takes real work to become and stay physically fit and that it is a sacrifice of time. Someone said that you don't pay a price for good health. You enjoy the benefits. How much better it is to stay as fit as possible than to have health problems, then to do something drastic to correct the problem? Fitness is a commitment. This commitment pays off in good health for the body and the mind. It affects how we feel about ourselves, and it affects our attitude.

I believe it was 1974 when my wife and I were on a trip to Hawaii with a group of Amoco service station operators (which we were also). While we were there, my wife took a picture of me side profile in my swimming suit. When we got home and were looking at the pictures, I wasn't very happy with what I saw. You get the picture! That picture was one of the better things that happened to me as it motivated me into action. I decided that I had to work out. I was committed to getting rid of that stomach. I was committed to exercise. Commitment means that you don't have to decide! If we are really committed, then the decision has already been made. My commitment to exercise has increased over time. I am more committed today than I was when I first started.

Our family life is definitely enhanced with a positive mental attitude. We look for the good in our family, not the points that are our weaknesses, which we have too, if we're honest with ourselves. The way we phrase things has a positive impact. We praise our children for what they do. We give them positive feedback. We are builders, not wreckers.

If we dress for success, then we apply a positive mental attitude to our work-place, our social contacts, our thinking, our spiritual life, our health, and our family life. We will enjoy the results.

Someone said that attitudes are like dandelion seeds, they spread and grow. Now, that is great if it's a positive attitude that we're spreading, but imagine the effects of spreading gloom and doom. Let's be spreaders of happiness and positive thoughts, ideas, and attitudes.

I just ran across an article in the bulletin of my Rotary Club from the summer of 1990. Now I couldn't probably find last week's, but this one I had filed away. I don't know who wrote this, but it is a dynamite message. If all of us would use this as our guide, we would be more effective human beings.

ATTITUDES ARE EVERYTHING
17 necessary ingredients for being effective with people

You will get what you want out of life only if you are able to get along with people. Getting along with others means that they like you and will do things for you. In other words, they react positively to your personality. Your personality is nothing more than attitudes in action. It is the way you communicate your thoughts about others and yourself. Here are some pointers to remember to make your personality pleasing, one that creates positive reactions in others.

1. **To have a friend, you must be one.**
2. **The greatest hunger that people have is to be needed, wanted, and loved.** Help create those feelings in others.
3. **Don't try to impress others.** Let them impress you.
4. **Be kind to people.** You can't always love them, but you can be kind to them.
5. **Learn to like yourself.** Others will respond to you the way you respond to yourself.
6. **Be enthusiastic.** Nothing significant was ever achieved without enthusiasm—including deep, rich human relationships.
7. **Be positive.** Positive people attract others; negative people repel others.
8. **Do things that make people feel important.** Write a letter. Give a compliment. Say "thank you." Praise. Encourage. Support. Cooperate.
9. **Sticking up for your rights is great, but do you always have to be right?**
10. **Be a good listener.** You can have a greater effect on others by the way you listen than by the way you talk.
11. **Unless you say something worthy about a person, say nothing.**
12. **Call a person by name.** Use it often in conversation.
13. **Communicate cheerfulness.** Smile. Be pleasant. Talk about the brighter things in life.
14. **Avoid arguments.**
15. **If you're going to make fun of someone, make sure it's you.**
16. **Help people like themselves.** The greatest compliment someone can give you is to say, "I like myself better when I'm with you."
17. **Be genuinely interested in others.** Get them to talk about themselves. Ask for their opinions, ideas, and viewpoints.

A positive mental attitude helps us to realize the abundance in our world. Two-thirds of the world is water teeming with fish and marine life of all kinds. We have huge forests full of birds and animals of all kinds. We look into the heavens, and we can't begin to count the stars. We live a world of abundance of all kinds. Are we placing limits on ourselves?

Look at the opportunities that we have in our vocations. We need to understand that if we're not where we want to be financially, then there are many options and opportunities for improving our lot. When we recognize the many opportunities presenting themselves to us and take the initiative to make things happen, they will happen. We have to stay positive and believe that we can achieve anything we want. In the process we may not accomplish exactly what we think we could or should on our time schedule. We need to keep on keeping on. Maybe we reach even greater heights than we thought we could accomplish, because as we believe and do, we become something that we were not before. Success breeds more success.

God made each one of us in a wonderful way, which is far beyond our comprehension. Yet we make the choices as to how we're going to use these capabilities. I think this relates well to Jesus' parable of the money that a master gave to his servants to invest during his long absence. On the master's return, they account for their investments. One did well, one fair, and the other nothing. The final statement tells the story. Jesus says, "to everyone who has something, more will be given, and he will have more than enough. But the person who has nothing, even that which he has will be taken away from him." In other words, if we don't use it we lose it. We can lose our resources and abilities. We have to know that we can accomplish what we want to. We can visualize in our mind's eye the achieving of our goals. When we can see it, we can achieve it. We affirm that we will win. We believe we can. It's a self-fulfilling prophecy. We need to visualize success, affirm that we can do it, and constantly believe.

A positive mental attitude is expecting the best, knowing that we will succeed in what we want to accomplish. PMA is seeing the good when something bad happens to us, knowing that out of what appears to be negative will come something even better. When something bad happens, thank God for it and really mean it, because you know that something even better is about to happen! We can wait with anticipation, wondering what God will do to, for, and through you. Live in anticipation!

A positive attitude is not loud and boisterous. A positive attitude attracts people to us; it does not drive people from us. A positive mental attitude is being bald (me), and feeling sorry for the people who have to spend so much time in grooming, blow drying, and combing their hair. PMA is feeling good about yourself, feeling that you are a winner, knowing that you can achieve and knowing what you want to be. You feel like you make a difference in the world in some way.

A positive mental attitude is a habit. It is a good habit, and habits make us or break us.

PMA is a great habit to develop. It is a way of life. Bad habits destroy us. Good habits build us up.

A positive attitude involves giving. It means giving of ourselves and our resources. Jesus said "Give and it will be given to you, good measure, pressed down, shaken together and running over will be put into your lap, for the measure that you use to give will be the measure that you get back." I believe that Jesus would not mean just financial resources, but also love, kindness, and anything positive that we share. Sharing comes from a positive attitude.

PMA dwells on abundance. We are thankful for what we have, whatever it is, and we concentrate on the abundance rather than just thinking about what we might lack. PMA looks at mistakes and failures as stepping stones, as positive experiences that prepare us for where we're going. We find some ways that don't work, and work on ways that do.

A positive attitude has direction. We are not just wandering around hoping that something works. Direction is provided by our goals and by working toward them.

We have to go around, over, or under our obstacles, but we keep going forward because we know that we can accomplish what we want. We keep moving in the right direction.

If a positive attitude is so effective, why isn't the progress that we make easier? In many cases we have been mentally conditioned all of our lives with negative thoughts and expectations: I hate Mondays. I was never good at that. I'm not very lucky. We procrastinate. We say, yes, I am going to do that someday. Don't keep procrastinating. Let this be the day to take action! Say to yourself, this is the first day of the rest of my life. I'm going to make the most of it. Do it. PMA is expecting the best outcomes. We go into a situation, and if we believe, really believe in positive outcomes, then our odds increase a thousand fold. We know we will succeed.

A positive mental attitude is:

1. **Expecting the best.**
2. **Knowing we will succeed.**
3. **Seeing the good when something bad happens.**
4. **Dwelling on abundance, not lack.**
5. **Looking at a mistake as a stepping stone.**
6. **A habit, a good habit, and our habits will either make us or break us.**

CHAPTER 16

Visualization

Visualization is the ability to picture mentally and to experience ideas, events, circumstances, and objects. In our everyday lives, we think in pictures. We can see ourselves and others in our minds. We can see things that happened to us in the past, and we can see ourselves in the future. This, of course, can be good or bad depending on our attitudes and dispositions. If we are negative, we are not going to like what we see. We can be defeated before we start. We can imagine all kinds of negative situations. We can see our fears play out before our very eyes. We can then say, I knew things were going to be bad. We can create our own problems. Visualization can make us or break us, depending on what we see happening in our lives mentally.

We, however, are positive people, so the pictures we see are positive in nature. Our future looks great. We do, though, have to be realistic about the options we see in the future so that we are ready to make the right choices. Visualizing in advance can keep us from making wrong choices.

When we can see in our mind's eye what we want to do or want to be, we have the opportunity to see options and make those right choices. We can create our own world through visualizing the future. In fact we can see our accomplishments before they ever happen, which keeps us on track to make our goals happen. We can live the life that we already saw in our minds.

If your goal is to be vice president of your company, see yourself doing what that vice president would be doing to be successful. Visualize your surroundings. Whose pictures are on the walls? They're your spouse and your children. Who else would be pictured on the wall other than your family? After all, this is YOUR office. Look around at all the plush surroundings and take it all in. Feel the smooth grain of your huge desk. Smell the fragrance of the furniture polish, yes, there's a lemon scent! Walk across the plush carpet and feel the carpet give under your feet.

Visualize what you would do as vice president. See yourself making important decisions. See the CEO of your company complimenting you for your great performance—and believe all this. So, how do you act? You act "as if" you are already the vice president. Yes, your duties may not have changed, but you have. You are decisive. Your performance and attitude are upbeat

You may already have a good job, but now you are ready to move up to the big time. As you make your decisions, you may ask yourself—what would a great vice president do under these circumstances? You are always supporting and advancing the cause of your company. By the way, you are not a clock watcher! You look at the clock at the end of the day and say to yourself, is it that time already? As you make decisions for your company, you are not thinking about how good or bad you would look, but is it the right thing to do? You are always thinking about how your decisions affect employees and the bottom line.

Keep a visualization board with pictures and positive statements that support your goals. Don't just put it up and forget it. Focus on it every day and visualize. Keep it up-to-date on what you really want. See it in your mind's eye.

My son Dean, when he was in college, wanted a new van and told me so. Now this wasn't very important to me, but it was to him. He knew that goal setting and visualization were important to me and an important part of my life, so he set out to play this game. He put a little green toy van on my desk with the word GOAL on it. Nothing happened. The next sign that went on it was SHORT TERM GOAL. Nothing happened.

The next sign was VERY SHORT TERM GOAL. He won. He got his van and guess what color it was. Green, of course! It either worked for him, or it got me conditioned, or both.

I had a visualization board in my office for years. It helped me to focus and follow through on my goals. Seeing one's goals visually is a real help in seeing and reaching the goals. Clip out pictures from magazines of things that you want or want to be. See yourself achieving goals that you have set or are thinking of setting. Let's get excited about making positive changes in your life. If we can see in it our minds, we can do it or be it!

An employee of 3M said, "I like to design machines. When I come to a point where I'm stymied and don't know what to do in the design, I visually (mentally) play with the machine. I mentally show it to my friends and explain it to them, and the answers come to me."

My uncle, Ted, who was somewhat of an inventor, said that as he was thinking about the design, he could potentially see the different parts of the machine and how they would turn. He could see how the gears meshed with each other. He could see this, all in his mind's eye. This was true visualization!

So, are you satisfied with where you're at? Are you getting satisfaction out of what you're doing? Are there some changes that should be made?

Don't stop here. Take action now. Act, don't put it off. Do it now. Let that be your slogan. Don't try to work on so many different goals at one time that you get frustrated. Peck away at them in every area of your life. Read good motivational books. You can control what you are! You can be what you want to be!

Develop the good habits of being enthusiastic, positive, and confident. You have the tools. You have the ability. Go for it!

CHAPTER 17

Potential

When we look at potential, we, first of all, should be looking at all the abundance in the world. Some two-thirds of the world is water filled with all kinds of fish and other kinds of marine life. Look at all the stars in the heavens. Think of all the oil and minerals underground. We do have an abundant world! Look at the human mind. It's a fantastic creation. What percentage of our potential do we use? Einstein said he used some 15 percent of his potential. What percentage do you think we use? We are sleeping giants when it comes to using our potential. Today is the day to realize it.

Our mind is a fantastic creation! We have a conscious and a subconscious mind. We are more aware of our conscious mind, with which we reason. We understand that we need to train our conscious mind. We fill it with facts and figures. We are schooled and educated to use our conscious mind. Yes, our conscious mind is very important, but our subconscious is very underused by most of us.

Our subconscious mind believes what we tell it. We need to constantly feed it what we want to get out of it. We need to affirm to our subconscious what we want to be true. If we believe in our mind that we are not very smart, we respond in real life just exactly that way. We tell ourselves that we are not capable of doing something and we can't. It's a self fulfilling prophecy. If we believe we can, we can. If we believe we can't, we can't. What we constantly feed our subconscious mind, good or bad, is what we get out of our subconscious mind.

Our subconscious mind is working 24 hours a day. If we can turn something that we need to solve over to our subconscious mind before we go to sleep, it can work for us while we sleep. There is power in our subconscious, day or night. We need to believe it, and we need to use it. We need to constantly have positive expectations. Someone said, "Anything that the mind can conceive and believe, it can achieve."

You may question your ability and capacity, but it is said that as humans we use at best 25 percent of our capabilities. Think of what we could do if we used 50 percent! The difference between a genius and us is that he or she knows it.

Zig Zigler, in his book *See You at the Top*, tells a story that goes something like this. Victor is 15 years old. He is doing very poorly in school. His teacher says that he is dumb. There is no use of his going to school any longer. It is a waste of time for him to do it. Victor's mother becomes convinced that the teacher is right. Victor leaves school and becomes an itinerate handyman getting any jobs that he can.

Seventeen years pass. Victor is now 32 years old. For some reason or other Victor is tested and the testing reveals that he has an IQ of 160. Victor is a genius! When Victor found out that he was a genius, he started performing like a genius. He started a successful businesses, he wrote books, and he even became the president of MENSA, an organization for geniuses.

Now I ask you, was Victor a genius all the time or did he become a genius overnight? I think you and I both know the answer to that question. He was a genius all the time, but for lack of confidence or low self-esteem, not feeling that he had anything to offer, he relegated himself to a life of underperformance. He didn't feel good about himself and believed the mistaken evaluation of his teacher.

Now I believe that many of us sell ourselves short on what we're capable of doing and what we are capable of becoming. I believe that each of us has some genius inside of us, something that few other people can do as well as we can. Yet we may say, I am not very smart, and we believe that lie just as Victor did. I say that it's up to each of us to work on that piece of genius that's inside us waiting to be called on. If each of us truly believed that we are at least a mini-genius, then we can make a difference in our lives and in the lives of others. I believe that God expects us to be all we can. We have to believe and do.

NOTES

CHAPTER 18

Friend or Foe?

W e have a friend who can make great things happen to us, or we have a foe who can do bad things to us. Who is this friend or foe who can do us good or bad? The friend or foe is one in the same. Our friend or foe is our subconscious mind, and it responds as friend or foe depending on the thoughts that we feed it.

Human beings are made in a fantastic way. Yes, we have a conscious mind, which is great in itself, but when we add to that our subconscious mind, we have a miracle. The subconscious mind controls us by the thoughts and ideas that we allow to enter it. If we have negative thoughts, the negatives control our lives. If we have positive thoughts, the positives control our lives.

As you manage your thoughts, you manage your life. We can react or respond to what happens positively or negative. It's within our control. How we respond to what happens to us is a habit. Responding positively is a good habit. Responding negatively is a bad habit. Our habits make us or break us. Unfortunately it seems that by nature we seem to be negatively conditioned, so it's our job to make new habits and change to being positively conditioned.

I believe that the subconscious mind is really a spiritual part of us. I believe that there are spiritual laws as real as the law of gravity (what goes up must come down). One of these laws is we attract to ourselves those things that we ask for and expect to get. Another spiritual law is the law of reciprocity (give and you will receive).

Our subconscious mind is task- or goal-oriented. When we know what we want (have a goal), our subconscious is like a guided missile homing in on the target (the goal). We don't need to fully understand our subconscious to use it. The more we use it, the more we will understand it.

CHAPTER 19

Affirmations

Affirmations are a tool that we can use to keep ourselves positive about our lives, about where we are going, and about changes we can make in ourselves. We need to grow our abilities, our self-esteem, our skills, our relationships, and our attitudes. There are many tools that we need to use to grow. Affirmations are declarations of what we believe to be true or what we want to believe is true. We can make much progress through the use of affirmations.

Affirmations have been called "self-talk." Affirmations are self-motivators, self-commands, or self-suggestions. It's feeding ourselves the positive results that we need and want. We need to feed our conscious and our subconscious mind positive data to keep us operating at the highest level we can in our lives. We need to use positive affirmations.

We use positive statements: I am a good sales person. I am a good mother or father. I am intelligent. I enjoy learning new things. I have a good personality. People like me. Whatever it is that we want to do or become, we need to affirm and believe. So what is it we want? We feed ourselves the right thoughts. Affirmations are positive conditioning. Yes, maybe we can't change ourselves completely overnight, but we can keep affirming and believing. Affirmations are a tool to lead us to what we want to be.

Do you have trouble talking to other people and don't really enjoy it? Say to yourself, "I really like to talk to other people." Notice that this affirmation is in the present tense. It's not "I will" in the future tense. Affirmations are always in the present tense. It's not "I will," it's "I am." Internalize that concept. You already own it. Believe. Look for opportunities to talk to others, and affirm that you enjoy it. You do, right?

Keep adding affirmations to your want list. Do affirmations like: People are interested in what I say. People are interested in me. I am confident. I am genuinely interested in other people. I like to learn and do new things.

For all of the characteristics or changes that we want to enjoy, we just add a new affirmation. Learning to use affirmations is just like learning to drive a car. When we establish the habit, we are on auto pilot. You may say "I am not being honest with myself, when I affirm something that I am not now." Affirmations are a tool to change our lives from where we are to where we want to be, and this is the process to make those wishes reality.

We can make affirmations for every area of our lives.

PHYSICAL	I am thin. I weigh xxx pounds. I exercise daily. I enjoy exercise.
SPIRITUAL	I read the Bible daily. I pray daily. I attend church.
SOCIAL	I have many friends. I enjoy people. Others really like me.
CAREER	I am ambitious. I earn xxx $ annually. I enjoy my work. I'm good!
MENTAL	I read books. I take classes. I'm intelligent. I learn new things.
FAMILY	I love my family. I enjoy family time.

How to form affirmations:

1. **Must be personal. Use the pronoun I.**
2. **Must be in present tense. (I am president of my company).**
3. **Must be stated positively.**
4. **Much more powerful if written.**

How to use affirmations:

1. **List them in a notebook. Read them in the morning or evening or several times a day.**
2. **Use note cards that you can strategically place, so that you're constantly reminded. You could even put it inside the refrigerator. Like, "I don't snack between meals."**
3. **Get very creative in your affirmations.**

We are constantly being bombarded by our television or radio about what we should do or not do. Shouldn't we be spending time thinking about what we want to do with our mind or our life? How about controlling our life with some affirmations? Always give yourself positive reinforcement. You can do whatever you want to do and believe you can do.

CHAPTER 20

Fear

recently heard a story about fear that puts the effects of fear in an appropriate perspective. The old lion, no longer agile and fast, cannot chase down the fleet animals. He does his part though by sitting in the middle of an area of tall grass and roaring loudly. This, of course, frightens the prey and they run away from the roar. This is where the young agile lions are in wait, and they quickly make "fast food" out of them.

The message and moral of this story is "run to the roar." The lion with that loud roar is weak and slow, which is the safest place for those fleet animals to be.

Many times our fears are completely unfounded. William James, renowned psychologist, said, "Do that which you fear and that is the death of fear." What are you afraid to do and why? How do you overcome this fear? You just do it! You do what you fear, and in most cases, you find that you never really had anything that you should have feared in the first place.

We have vivid imaginations that allow us to expect the worst out of situations. When we make positive moves to face the fears, we realize how foolish we were to hold back and not go forward with all the gusto we could muster.

The feeling of victory as we overcome the fears that have gripped us in the past will far outweigh our false fears. As we have success after success in overcoming our small fears, we become a new person with the confidence to succeed in anything we want to do.

So, of what are you afraid? Whatever it is, it is rarely real. They say that many people are more afraid of public speaking than of death itself. How do you overcome that fear? You just do it. Do you want some help? Take a Dale Carnegie Training course. You'll come out of that training with some new ideas and confidence. You may say that costs money. Well, it's worth it!

Here's another suggestion. Join a Toastmasters club. There's a Toastmasters club not too far away from you. In your weekly Toastmasters meeting you'll have a chance every meeting in one way or another to be on your feet in front of your fellow members. That's what it takes: repetition. If you will stick it out for four sessions, then you'll be well on your way to being comfortable speaking in front of groups. You also get evaluated by your peers, and they will offer suggestions to improve your speaking ability. You will evaluate them, too!

I joined a Toastmasters club around 17 years ago with the idea that I would do it for a year to "learn all there was to know about public speaking." I'm still there. I do a fair amount of public speaking to Rotary Clubs and other groups. I still go to my Toastmasters club regularly, because that way I never get out of practice. If there is a long lapse of time between speeches, then you can lose your edge.

Toastmasters also gives you a chance to try out a speech that you will be giving to another group in front of a friendly supportive audience. The group can give you suggestions on how you might improve your presentation.

If you want to be a good golfer or tennis player, you have to practice. They say that practice makes perfect, but you've got to be practicing the right stuff. I can personally say that this is true in my case when playing tennis. I don't take lessons, so I just keep doing the same mistakes over and over again. (At least I get exercise!) Someone said, "If you do what you've always done, you'll get what you always got." So are we happy with the results we're getting? Are we hanging back and not getting the results we want because of unfounded fears. Let's not keep doing the same old things. Let's make some changes. This is true of speaking also. I can assure you that if you want to be a good speaker, you can do it.

No matter what it is that we would like to do, but hesitate because of unfounded fears of some kind, we can overcome it. As William James said, and I again repeat it, "Do that which you fear and that is the death of fear."

NOTES

CHAPTER 21

Be All That You Can Be

Some time ago there was a slogan, "Be all that you can be. Join the Army." Now I'm not suggesting that we have to join the army to "be all that we can be." All of us down deep would like to be all that we can be. We all want to be successful in our lives, but where do we start and what do we do?

A lot of what I have to say about being all we can be is that we need to develop the art of asking. The art of asking is just doing it. We have to overcome our shyness of asking for things and opportunities. If we don't ask and expect to receive, then we have no one to blame but ourselves. We have to do some asking to get from where we're at to where we want to be in life. All of us have areas in which we're reluctant to ask. If we just ask for anything that we want, we will find that we get our fair share, and the asking gets easier and easier.

We have to make sure that we're thinking big when we ask for something. When we ask and expect to get what we're asking for, we may as well be thinking big and abundant rather than something small and limited. We often have a tendency to think too small and maybe even negative. Negative thoughts like, "I know I'll never get that," should have no place in our minds. If we believe we can, we can. If we believe we can't, we can't. It is the self-fulfilling prophecy.

Another quote goes like this, "Ask and you will receive, seek and you will find, knock and it will be opened to you. For he who asks will receive, he who seeks, finds, and to him who knocks the door will be opened." In case you didn't recognize that quote, it comes from the Bible and is spoken by none other than Jesus Christ, who would seem like pretty good authority. We need to be in the habit of asking, because when we ask, things happen. As the saying goes, we have to get our ASK in gear. We need to ask, and we need to believe that what we ask for happens.

We need to overcome the fear of asking or of whatever it is that is holding us back from asking. We guys seem to have the genetic disposition to not ask for directions, even when we don't have a clue about where we are. Just think of all the time and frustration we could have avoided if we had just asked.

We have to keep asking for anything that we want or need. Maybe what we need to do is just to keep asking for every little thing that crosses our mind to establish the habit of asking. Asking is a great habit to develop. Let's make asking our new most important habit.

We need to seek. We have asked, now we really have to start digging in to make what we asked for happen. Jack Canfield in his book *The Success Principles* writes about what he does to become more effective in what he does. He may have just finished presenting a seminar, and he might ask a participant to evaluate his performance on a scale of 1–10 with 10 being the best. If the person responds with an 8, Jack would say, "what would it take in your mind and opinion for my presentation to be a 10." Now he has to be prepared to listen to what that person has to say. That person may have a very valid point that would make that rating jump to a 10. How much more effective would his next seminar be with that improvement added?

I was going to be giving a 30-minute talk to a group of incoming Rotary Club presidents, so I decided to try out a condensed version on my Toastmaster club the week before the meeting for presidents elect. It was to be a motivational talk. In the talk I was hitting heavily on the value of asking, asking, and more asking. As I finished my talk, I decided I would use Jack Canfield's technique of asking for a rating and then the question of what would it take to be a 10.

In Toastmasters we always have each member evaluate and critique the speaker in writing with one oral evaluator. Two of the written evaluations were very interesting to me as I felt that they were probably saying the same thing. One just used one word that I picked up on. The word was humility. The other comment was a question. Don't you think any of us ask? The message that I picked up on this was that I was coming off as one who thought I was superior. I was sure including myself in what I was saying, but it obviously didn't come off that way. That was valuable information to me to prepare for my real presentation of that subject. I don't believe I would have got that feedback if I had not asked, "what would it take to make my talk a 10?"

So how can we use this Jack Canfield technique in our everyday life? You go to your boss for your quarterly evaluation. You ask him to evaluate you on a scale of 1–10. He says you're an 8. You ask what would it take for you to rate me a 10? He says that you don't seem to take enough initiative; you do good work but wait to do as you are told. Now you know what to work on. You initiate. You make things happen. You go in to the next evaluation with confidence and you get that 10 rating, and with it comes more responsibility and compensation. You may have a company that you supply, but you know you are not getting all the business from them you should. You ask them how they rate you, and you ask what would it take for me to be a 10 in your eyes? You do what they say would make you a 10. As you prove yourself to them, your sales improve. You know what they want and you deliver.

CHAPTER 22

Don't Believe
All Those Lies

From when I was a teenager, I remember a popular song that went something like this: "Don't believe all those lies, darling just believe your eyes, and look, look my heart is an open book. I love nobody but you!" You may say, what does that have to do with anything? Really, it doesn't maybe, but it's my introduction to the fact that we shouldn't believe all the lies that we are told or fed throughout our lifetime. Some of these (lies) statements may have been told to us directly or subtly implied, ending up giving us the idea that we are limited in what we are capable of achieving in life. Maybe others can do it, but not us. That's a lie!

People may, for some reason or other, prefer to tell us what we can't do, rather than encouraging us to succeed. So they tell us these lies. They are lies that would limit our ability and our success if we believe them. We can have enough doubts about what our capabilities are, without the "help" we get from others. Many times they may be envious of what someone is accomplishing, so they can tell you about all the people who tried and failed. Don't believe their lies! Also, don't believe the lies that we tell ourselves that would discourage us from doing what we want to do.

So what are these lies? You never graduated from college, so you're not smart enough. Your family always struggled financially, so what makes you think that you can do better? Your I.Q. is not high enough. You don't have enough money to get started in business. You don't have the right connections. It takes money to make money. You would certainly fail, so why try? All the various lies could go on for pages and pages. Don't stay on the sidelines just because someone else says that you can't succeed. I repeat, don't believe all those lies!

We have a tendency to belittle ourselves, and we believe all the lies that we are fed. We seem ready to believe all those lies that we and others feed our subconscious. We feed ourselves ideas like you are too old. You are too young. You can never achieve what you want to. You failed once and you will fail again. You made a big mistake and you can never recover. You will never amount to much. You can never be forgiven. You're not good enough. You just can't do it. You're not a good learner. Nobody loves me. We could go on and on with all the negativity.

The real fact is that we can overcome these lies. It is within our control. We can make our own choices. We can choose to think and believe the positives. We are in control. It's up to each of us to overcome the negative messages that we receive. If we believe we can, we can! We can do anything that we set our mind to.

Every day we have a decision to make. Am I going to believe all those lies, or am I going to step out and be positive? Whatever our circumstances, we make a choice. The choice is ours. Things may not look very good for us on paper, but we can still choose what our mental attitude is going to be. Our thinking makes it so.

NOTES

CHAPTER 23

Communication

H ow clearly do we communicate to others and with others? Have you ever had a situation where you had communicated a message to someone else that you thought was very clear and concise, only to find out that the other person had misunderstood you? This, of course, is happening every day.

A friend of mine had a teenage daughter who was looking for a job. She interviewed at a business and was hired. The employer told her to report for work for her training ten to three the next day. When she showed up for work at ten minutes to three the next day, they asked her where she had been. They told her that she was supposed to have been at work from ten in the morning until three in the afternoon. Oops!

Think about the number of mistakes that have happened because of this kind of unclear information. In this story, maybe it's no big deal, although she could have lost out in getting the job. Just think of the big problems that can be caused by this kind of communication.

A situation similar to that happened to me many years ago. We started having a problem with cash shortages at one of my gasoline service stations, so obviously we have to get to the bottom of that problem. After all, it's not always easy to make money anyway, and if you have some employee who wants to be your partner without any investment, that is a problem! To try to solve this situation I told an employee, be sure, no matter how busy we are at noon, to check out. What I meant was to do a cut off on the cash register and read the pump meters to determine that our cash was all accounted for.

I was at another one of my stations when I got a call from an employee at the first station saying that this employee had left at noon. The employee that left had interpreted what I said to mean that he should 'check out' or, in other words, leave for the day. As you look at this, you can probably see who the poor communicator was. ME. I had to go find the employee to get him back to work.

This kind of situation happens because of fuzzy language or a possible double meaning. It should make us more aware of how we need to listen. Then if it is not clear to us, to make sure we ask the right questions to get the right answers. It can save us a lot of grief.

This subject is probably something that should be aimed at me. I don't listen the way I should. Now if you think I'm exaggerating, don't take my word for it, just ask my wife.

NOTES

CHAPTER 24

On Giving

Giving is a way of life. Giving is as important to the giver as to the receiver, probably even more so. There is something special about the feeling that you have when you give. A stingy, non-giving person does not realize the joy that comes from giving. One of the benefits of being a giver comes from the law of reciprocity, which means give and you will receive. It's really a law of nature, which I would say is God.

Jesus said in Luke 6:38 "Give, and it will be given to you: good measure, pressed down, shaken together, and running over, will be put into your bosom. For with the same measure that you use, it will be measured back to you." In the Old Testament of the Bible, Malachi 3:10, God says "Bring all the tithes into the storehouse, that there may be food in my house, and try Me now in this." Says the Lord of hosts, "If I will not open for you the windows of heaven and pour out for you such blessing that there will not be room enough to receive it."

Giving is an important issue with Mary and me. Each of us makes a difference in the world by our commitment to give. It's through giving that we feel connected to being a small part of the things that are happening in our church and in the world. It was something like the early 1970s when Mary and I went with the senior pastor from our church to a church leadership seminar at what is now the Crystal Cathedral in Garden Grove, California. The seminar was led by Robert Schuller, founder and senior pastor of the cathedral. It was while we were there that we committed to giving at least 10 percent of our income to helping others. I feel that we have been blessed as a result of this commitment.

Mary and I feel that we have been very blessed, and we feel good about giving of our resources to further the spread of the gospel and to share with other organizations that make a difference in the world. We no longer look at giving the tithe, but at going well beyond that. We believe that The Rotary

Foundation is instrumental in making our world a better place. I may talk about percentages of income that we give, but we are not limited by the 10 percent or the 20 percent; it's about being a part of something that is bigger than we are. I sincerely believe that we can't out-give what God has done for us.

It must have been about the year 2000 when we were having a fund drive to build a much larger church on a new location a few miles away from our old church, Lord of Life Lutheran in Maple Grove, Minnesota. So, naturally we had to have a fund drive to make that happen. Mary and I decided to give an eleven-unit apartment building that we owned in the city of Saint Paul to our church and to The Rotary Foundation. We did a charitable remainder unitrust that included both organizations. The two entities had to jointly own the property until it was sold. We could have no control over the price for which it would be sold or have any involvement in the transaction. It was completely out of our hands at that point.

The property sold quickly. The proceeds were then distributed, one-third in cash to the church. They needed the money to build. The two-thirds that went to The Rotary Foundation was set up in the charitable remainder trust (to do good in the world).

The benefits include feeling good about making a difference in the world. Then there was a good tax deduction. (That's always good!) The two-thirds that went to The Rotary Foundation is in a trust that pays Mary and me seven per cent interest annually, paid quarterly until the last of Mary and I die. (Let's not make it too soon!)

My Rotary club is in Roseville, Minnesota. About 11 years ago, I took over as the person who does the asking for money for The Rotary Foundation for our club. We had been raising about $10,000 a year, which I felt was way below where we should be in giving for the potential that was in the club. I gave a Rotary Foundation talk to the group, and then I did something that really scared me, because I didn't know what the reaction would be. They could react negatively and say, who does Jerry think he is, or they could respond positively.

What I did was to say that I would give one thousand dollars to The Rotary Foundation for each member that would give one thousand dollars, up to ten thousand dollars. The response was great. I had to give the ten thousand dollars! It was successful and our club has been a leader in total and per capita giving in our district of sixty-six clubs ever since. We have eighty-four members in our club. We went over thirty thousand dollars that first year. We have been in the mid-thirties regularly, and we are around forty-five thousand dollars in 2007. It pays to ask!

I'm always involved in Rotary and in my church to ask others to give, and I feel that it is important to give. I also believe that if we're going ask others to give that we need to "lead the way." By the way, that was the theme of the 2006–2007 year in Rotary. We have to lead by example.

I believe it was in 1985 that I was doing some fairly major remodeling to a building we owned that is an automotive parts store. I needed to do a loan and the loan officer was a nice young lady. Of course I had to give her a copy of my income taxes to verify income. Twenty years later, she told me that she always liked to take a look at business people's charitable giving in relation to their income. She said that after looking at what I gave, she had set a goal to equal that. Recently she told me that she had now accomplished that. It makes me feel good to have had some positive influence on someone, especially someone who I had no idea that I would impact at all. Others watch what we do, whether we're aware of it or not.

Years ago, at a church that I no longer belong to, another member and I were out to make some of the easy calls asking for the pledge. You kind of start out with the easy calls so you can have a quick impact. The two of us then were going to make this easy "ask," but before we could get started this guy became rather hostile and said, "I give a lot of money. Why don't you ask those that aren't good givers?" Then he turned on us and said, "how much do you give?" Fortunately we both gave more than he did, but evidently he felt he was giving more than his share. If we're asking, we'd better lead by example.

In 1996 a gentleman died who was scheduled to be the district governor of another close-by Rotary District in just six months. I didn't know him well, but by the time I heard all the stories about him, I felt it was my loss. He was a fund raiser of large gifts. At the funeral, they quoted John, the deceased, as saying, "Everyone has a yearning to give, they just don't know it, you have to help them."

Why do people give? There are many different answers to that question. I don't suppose that I could come up with all the reasons why people give. There may be some that give for reasons I've never thought of. I guess I can only answer for myself. I give because I enjoy giving. I give because it's the right thing to do. I give to make a difference in people's lives in many ways. I give because the Bible says give and you will receive. I give because it feels good. I give because I expect others to give, and if I ask them to give, I had better lead the way. I give because I feel so blessed in every area of my life. I give because it helps spread the word of God.

Have you ever given because of the recognition that you receive from the organization involved? We probably all have been influenced at one time or another to give at a certain level for some recognition that we might get. I would like to be able say that I've never been influenced by recognition that one might get, but it just might not be entirely true. We human beings have our weaknesses!

CHAPTER 25

Prayer

Most of us try to solve our own problems. Maybe we need a new job. Maybe we need a new or different relationship. Maybe we need more resources of one kind or another. All of us at one time or another need some healing of the mind. Maybe we are worried about our own health or that of someone else. There are many kinds of stress with which we have to deal.

Read (and listen) to this Bible passage from Philippians 4:4–8. "Rejoice in the Lord always. Again I say rejoice! Let your gentleness be known to all men. The Lord is at Hand. BE ANXIOUS FOR NOTHING, but in everything by prayer and supplication, with thanksgiving, let your request be made known to God; and the PEACE OF GOD WHICH SURPASSES ALL UNDERSTANDING, will guard your hearts and minds through Christ Jesus."

Finally, brethren, whatever things are true, whatever things are noble, whatever things are just, whatever things are pure, whatever things are lovely, whatever things are of good report, if there is any virtue and if there is anything praiseworthy–meditate on these things.

I had been going through a stressful time with some illnesses in the family, some business issues, and the like. It's easy during times like this to wake up at night and break out in a sweat thinking about problems. It doesn't solve anything, and it certainly affects your sleep negatively.

I read the passage in the Bible that I just quoted, and it seemed to fit what I needed. I decided that this would be my Bible reading every day. I memorized the passage. At night as a problem would come into my mind, I could tell myself to be ANXIOUS FOR NOTHING and turn it over to God "in prayer and supplication with thanksgiving." IT WORKS!

So the message of this passage is the following list and more.

1. **Rejoice in the Lord. Be thankful.**
2. **Let your relationship with God show.**
3. **Be anxious for nothing. Turn it over to God.**
4. **Ask with thanksgiving, knowing that God will open the doors you need opened.**
5. **Tell God your concerns.**
6. **Experience His Peace.**
7. **Meditate on the positive, praiseworthy things. In other words, dwell on the positive; don't dwell on the negative.**

Jesus encourages us to ask and believe that we will receive that for which we asked. In John 16: 23–24, Jesus says "I say to you, whatever you ask the Father in my name, He will give you. Until now you have asked for nothing in my name. Ask and you will receive, that your joy may be full." Jesus wants us to ask! What do you need? Pray about it. In John 14:11–14, Jesus says, "and whatever you ask in My name, that will I do, that the father may be glorified in the Son. If you ask anything in my Name, I will do it." In Mark 11:24, Jesus says "therefore, I say to you, whatever things you ask when you pray, believe that you *receive* them, and you will have them." Notice the word receive in italics. Receive is in the present tense. Believe that you already have it and you will receive it. We could go on and on with examples of Jesus asking us to ask.

Does God answer prayer? When I was in a sales training course with Standard Oil Company in 1960, one of my assignments was to be a mystery driver. As a mystery driver, I was to check out appearance and cleanliness of the service stations as well as to check out the level of service that the attendant gave. Just in case you have forgotten, there was a time when good service was mandatory. We had to check the oil, clean the windows, vacuum the car, check air in the tires, and on and on.

Obviously I had to look like a real customer, so I had to buy gas. So how do I get rid of the gas? I had a crank pump, which could pump the gas out of the car into five-gallon cans. I had something like 5 five-gallon cans. After leaving and pumping out five gallons, I would be ready for the next stop and could ask for a fill, which, of course, would be five gallons.

Soon all the cans are full and the car is full, so I had to get rid of the gas. The answer is to find someone with a car to whom I could offer free gas. Now that may sound real easy, but people are a little suspicious of what the catch is, and is this good gas? But a lot of people like to get something for nothing, so I could unload it.

So what I'm building up to is that I have everything full and I need to get rid of it. I find two guys working on loading a van. I stop and get out to ask the guys if they would like some free gas. They just stopped and looked at each in almost disbelief. Then they told me their story. They were pastors or workers for a struggling church. They had no money and very little gas in their tank, and they had a fairly long drive to get the stuff they were hauling to another church location. They had prayed that God would provide for them. God answered the prayer, and I was the answer to their prayer.

Have you ever prayed that you would be the answer to the prayer of someone else. I have prayed that God would make me the answer to someone else's prayer. It can be somewhat empowering, as you never know if the opportunity presented itself and you blew it, or could it be that you said the right word to the right person that needed it and you never knew that you were the answer to that person's prayer.

Think about it. How would we treat all the people with whom we come into contact if we were indeed looking and hoping that we would be the answer to their prayer? I would challenge each of us to go about our day's work or play with the thought and prayer that today might be the day.

CHAPTER 26

Goals

A goal is a destination: someone said, "what you get by reaching your destination is not nearly as important as what you become by reaching your destination." As we work toward our goals, we have successes and we may have failures, but when we are persistent and stick to pursuing our goals at all costs, we become a stronger and a more confident person. The successes that we enjoy as a result of our efforts and strategies give us even more assurance that we are indeed winners.

Paul Meyer of Success Motivation Institute said, "crystallize your thinking. If you're not making the progress you want to make and are capable of making, it's because your goals are not clearly defined." We need to have written plans as it keeps us on track, blocks out distractions, measures progress, and helps us to overcome procrastination, fear, doubt, and worry. Deadlines alert body chemistry, and we act with a sense of urgency.

When we set goals, we should dream big and set big goals. I read a story of an editor of a newspaper in a city in Oklahoma. He had been a paper boy with a desire and a dream to become an editor. Thirty years later he's an editor. He has received awards and has accomplished many dreams. A magazine did a story about the editor and said that it was fantastic to dream a dream so young and accomplish it. The editor said no, it was a tragedy. You see, I could just as well have dreamed about being the editor of the *New York Times*, and accomplished that. The message is, why dream small dreams? Why set small goals?

J.C. Penney, founder of the J.C. Penney Company, said, "Give me a stock clerk with a goal, and I will give you a man who will make history. Give me a man without goals, and I will give you a stock clerk."

Most people have been exposed to goal setting to one degree or another. One way to make sure that we are setting goals the way that helps us get the best results is to use SMART goals, which we have already discussed.

So what is it that we may have wanted to do at one time, but we decided that there's no way we could make that goal because it just looked too big and maybe even impossible. It's a new day. We have grown. We are not the same person that we used to be. Maybe now is the time to take a look at that goal. Maybe today is the day! Let's go for it!

NOTES

CHAPTER 27

Do It Now!

An African Mauri man said, "a man with no legs should get on the ox before it gets up." We have opportunities that show up for us many times in every area of our lives. When the opportunity comes, are we ready to take action and do it now? As in the proverb of the man with no legs, we have to be ready when the opportunity presents itself.

How many times have we had the chance to do something, but we didn't think we were quite ready yet. We can come up with all kinds of excuses why it just isn't the right time yet. We may ask and pray for a certain break, and when it comes, we let it pass us by for one reason or another. We may think that later is better because we don't want to take that big step to do it now. We may procrastinate because we think of all the potential risk in what we want to do. We have to be like the legless man and take advantage of the opportunity when it presents itself for a limited time.

That doesn't mean that everything we run across that looks like an opportunity is blindly acted on. Everything that looks like a great opportunity is not necessarily so. Just because something looks great does not necessarily mean that it's suited for our individual skill sets.

We have to realize that an opportunity that we have is not something that lasts forever. We, also, must make sure that we do the "due diligence" to make sure the opportunity is real and the right fit. What is the right fit? How do we know what the right fit is for us? In some cases we may have some doubts about making a big business decision. We have to ask ourselves what is the worst thing that can happen to us as a result of our decision? Can we live with it? When we are comfortable (at least half-way comfortable) with our decision, it's time to take action. Yes, we can make a wrong decision, but if thought out carefully, we should know where the risks are, and also the opportunities.

As an aside, and an important aside, we have to make sure that our spouse buys in with a decision that can materially affect the future of the family. This also means that we have to do our homework and due diligence to insure our success. But nothing happens until we just do it. Is it time to get on the ox?

NOTES

CHAPTER 28

Persistence

Five guys who were engineering types, ages around forty-five, decided to go into business together. They chose to apply their technical experience toward starting a new company to develop high-altitude balloons and other inflatables for the United States government. Now, this sounded like a pretty sure bet, after all, what would be more secure than contracts with the government? They named the company Pentair. The reason for the name was "penta" for five, the number of founders. The "air" was for the air inflatables and balloons they would manufacture.

No sooner did they quit their jobs and become entrepreneurs than the government decided to divert all development funds to the Vietnam war effort. There went the balloon business! There also went the partnership. They struggled to secure capital by incorporating and selling stock in their company. In the scramble to develop a new business, one of the founders contracted cancer and died, and three of the others decided to seek their fortunes elsewhere. Just one person of the original five hung on and pursued new ventures to salvage the company. This person who persevered is Murray Harpole. Murray is a friend and a member of the same Rotary Club to which I belong.

The fortunes of the company improved with the purchase of a bankrupt paper mill in Wisconsin. Its successful turnaround led to further acquisitions in the then-troubled paper industry. At the end of six years, the company had achieved stability and the suggestion of a good future. This achievement was due in large part to Mr. Harpole and his family, who made a commitment at the outset to devote five years to the venture, no matter how difficult it became.

The company continued to grow and develop. Today, forty years after its founding, Pentair, Inc. operates on a global scale with 15,000 employees and annual sales of three billion dollars.

The message is that persistence and commitment are major elements of success.

I read an account of the old-time swimming great, Florence Chadwick. In 1952 she was to swim from Catalina Island to the California coast, some twenty-one miles away. The waters were icy cold. After fifteen hours she was tired and later asked to be taken out of the water. She later found out that she was only a half hour from shore. She now knew that she could have made it if she had realized how close she was to reaching her goal.

Two months later she decided to make the swim again. Again she couldn't see because of the fog, but this time she had faith that she could make it all the way, and she did. She was the first woman to swim the channel, and she beat the record by two hours.

You may not be able to see the light at the end of the tunnel, but it is there. Keep going!

How about this persistent character? He failed in business at age twenty-two. Ran for the legislature and was defeated at age twenty-three. He failed again in business at age twenty-four. He was elected to the legislature at age twenty-five. His sweetheart died when he was twenty-six. He had a nervous breakdown at age twenty-seven. He was defeated for speaker at twenty-nine years of age. He was defeated as elector at age thirty-one. He was defeated for Congress when he was thirty-four. He was elected to Congress at age thirty-seven. He was defeated for congress when he was thirty-nine. He was defeated for Senate at forty-six. He was defeated for vice president at age forty-seven. He was again defeated for Senate at age forty-nine. He was elected as president of the United States when he was fifty-one. This man was Abraham Lincoln. Persistence paid off for Abe Lincoln.

We had a young Laotian man speak to our Rotary Club. He came from a war-torn area. He had been in the United States for eight years when I talked to him. He spoke English well. He had graduated from high school and already had done two years in college. He was an Eagle Scout, and you have to accomplish this feat by age eighteen, so he was obviously on the fast track ever since he arrived in the United States.

I asked how he accomplished so much in such a short period of time. He goes back in time to war times, and he said, "when the bombs come down, you lay down and then run, run, run, and get there. Now I don't worry about the process, I just want to get there!" He knew what persistence was all about. Are you and I that persistent and committed?

The following poem by an unknown author says volumes about persistence.

Don't Quit

> **When things go wrong as they some times will,**
> **When the road you're trudging seems all uphill,**
> **When the funds are low and the debts are high,**
> **And you want to smile, but you have to sigh,**
> **When care is pressing you down a bit—**
> **Rest if you must, but don't you quit.**
>
> **Life is queer with its twists and turns,**
> **As everyone of us sometimes learns.**
> **And many a fellow turns about**
> **When he might have won had he stuck it out.**
> **Don't give up though the pace seems slow—**
> **You may succeed with another blow.**
>
> **Often the goal is nearer than**
> **It seems to a faint and faltering man;**
> **Often the struggler has given up**
> **When he might have captured the victor's cup;**
> **And he learned too late when the night came down,**
> **How close he was to the golden crown.**
>
> **Success is failure turned inside out—**
> **The silver tint of the clouds of doubt,**
> **And you can never tell how close you are,**
> **It may be near when it seems afar;**
> **So stick to the fight when you're hardest hit,—**
> **It's when things seem worse that you mustn't quit.**

CHAPTER 29

Choices

Every day we have choices and decisions to make. We can choose to be happy, or we can choose to be unhappy. We may have circumstances that are not easy to deal with. We all have times when we may wish that circumstances and situations were different. We can then choose to feel sorry for ourselves, or we can choose to overcome whatever the situation is. We have a choice. The choice is ours. Things may not look so good on paper, but we can still choose what our mental attitude will be.

So how do you feel? Well, I have this little ache and I think I'm coming down with a cold. You're right, you talked yourself into it. My habit has been when I start to come down with a cold, I tell myself that I'm getting over a cold. If some one asks me if I am coming down with a cold, I say "no, I'm getting over a cold." It makes a difference.

We can feed our minds positives or negatives. The way we think affects the outcomes in our lives. We may say, "I can only believe what the facts are." You can't change the facts. The facts may seem real, but what and the way we think, positive or negative, affects the facts and the outcomes.

Habits can make us or break us. I would say that one of the best things that we can do for ourselves and our lives is to commit to the habit of positive thinking. It seems to be more natural for us to look at things negatively. We can change our choices and change our lives.

A friend's e-mail says, "life is full of choices; choices have consequences."

CHAPTER 30

Motivation

Paul Meyer of Success Motivation Institute defined motivation as goal-directed action. (We know what we want, and we take action steps to achieve the goal.) He also defines motivation as a desire held in expectation with the belief that it will be realized. He said there are three kinds of motivation: 1. Fear—We do something out of fear because there are negative consequences if we don't do them or at least we may feel that there are negative consequences. Obviously fear is not the way we like to be motivated. It sure can get you motivated if you're in a tough or dangerous spot. 2. Incentive—We do something because there are positive consequences if we do them. This would be the good stuff. Maybe it's recognition or a higher salary. 3. Attitude—Attitude comes from the inside. We know we can achieve. We feel it. Bring on any challenge. We're ready for it. Being motivated attitudinally is a great way to live. We're having fun and reaping the rewards that goes with the success we are achieving.

When we are motivated attitudinally we can make big things happen in our lives. We are not living in fear. We believe we can achieve anything that we want to and have fun doing it. We have the enthusiasm and optimism to look for challenges for us to tackle. Yes, it may still take a lot of work to get to our goal, and, yes, there may be setbacks along the way, but we know that if we believe and if we keep our eyes on the goal, we will make it happen.

The most productive type of motivation is the kind that is generated from the inside. Others may try to motivate us to do what they want us to do, or what they think we should do, or something that would benefit them if we were to do it. True motivation comes from the inside and expresses itself in the form of outside results.

CHAPTER 31

Resentment

Have you ever had a situation where you felt that you were mistreated or wronged by someone? How did you respond to the situation? How did you feel about the incident? Did you feel like you really wanted to get your hands on that person? Resentment can build up and destroy your peace of mind. You can't get over how you felt about what the person did to you. To make matters worse, the person that you feel wronged you doesn't seem to be concerned at all.

So what do you do to get over how you feel about the situation? Do you keep harboring the negative feelings? These resentments and grudges can just eat away at you, if you let them.

I heard a story of a milkman who delivered milk on a regular route. The milkman was responsible for collecting the money the customer owed, and if he didn't collect the money, it came out of his pocket. He had this one lady as a customer that owed him seventy-nine dollars that was past due. He tried to collect, but wasn't successful. He went to her house again and she had moved. He was bitter and told some of his other customers about it.

A woman on his route was aware of his bitterness about the situation. She told him to give her the $79 dollars. What she was trying to say was that this resent-ment was really eating away at him and that he had to mentally let it go. In his mind he had to not feel that she had stiffed him, but that he had given the money to her.

He took the lady's advice and got over the issue. He was working a route as a substitute in a different neighborhood and delivered to this old customer. She came running out and apologized to the milkman. She tried to give him a twenty dollar bill. The milkman said something like, "you don't owe me any money, I already gave it to you." He had mentally let go and got over his resentment at being stiffed.

So how about you and me, do we have people who have done something to us for which we have never forgiven them? Isn't it time to let go? Isn't it time to forgive? Life is too short to live with grudges and resentments. Maybe it's time to write a letter, to make a phone call, or to knock on someone's door. You might be surprised by the wonderful reception. Go for it!

This might be the right time to ask for forgiveness of someone who was wronged by you or thought they were wronged by you. It doesn't really make any difference who was right or who was wrong. Even if you know the other person was wrong, say you're sorry for what you said or did. Make it a time of healing. Even if you fail in the reconciliation, you will feel good about the way you handled it. When the great Scorer comes to score the game, you will have won regardless of the results.

NOTES

CHAPTER 32

A B C D E F
Of Walking On Water

I n 1987, my wife, Mary, and I went on a tour of Israel with a group of around 30 people from our church and another Lutheran church. One of the events was a cruise on the Sea of Galilee. Before we went on the cruise our pastor asked me to lead a devotional meditation while we were on the boat. As we were cruising on the Sea, we were being told of the ministry of Jesus, and the spot was pointed out where he had fed the 5,000 people.

You had the feeling that you were indeed floating on holy water. The boat came to a stop in the middle of the Sea. The engine was shut off, and there was a holy silence. Our group was on the top deck, and the others on the cruise were below. As I began the devotional, I couldn't help but say, "this is the day the Lord has made, let us rejoice and be glad in it!"

Contrast that peaceful scene with what had happened on this same Sea some 2,000 years before. The night was dark, windy, stormy, and scary. Jesus' disciples were in a boat that was getting beaten up by the storm. Suddenly they saw something that looked to them like a ghost walking on the water, and they were more afraid. As the figure got closer, Peter yelled out, "Master if that is you, command that I should come to you." Jesus said, "Come." Peter started walking across the water. Then the account in the Bible said, "he saw the wind and he was afraid and he began to sink and Peter said to Jesus 'save me' and Jesus reached out and rescued him."

We recently had a Bible study for small groups in our church that was based on the book *If You Want to Walk on Water, You've got to get out of the Boat*. It helped us to think about our comfort zones (staying in the boat) and realizing that if we're really going to change and improve, then we have to be willing, like Peter, to get out of the boat. We have to do things that we have never done before.

YOU CAN PAINT YOUR OWN WORLD

All of us are familiar with learning the ABC's. Now I'm going to suggest some ways that we can use to become water walkers.

I will call them the ABCDEF's of Water Walking.

The A is for ask.
The B is for believe.
The C is for commit.
The D is for do.
The E is for expect.
The F is for focus.

ASK We will never accomplish anything significant unless we are willing to ask. If we want someone to buy something, we have to ask for the sale. If there's something that we want someone else to do, we have to ask them to do it. People can't read our minds; we have to ask. It seems like too many of us are timid about asking.

Recently I heard or read a story that went like this. Joe Smith dies and goes to heaven where, of course, he is met by St. Peter, who will show Joe all around heaven. They start out and he sees all kinds of great golden buildings. Joe is impressed, but all of the sudden he notices a big building that looks like a gigantic warehouse. Joe asks Peter what that building is. Peter says that Joe wouldn't want to know because it would just make him sad. Joe says that he really wants to know what it is, but Peter prevails and they go on. Everything is even better than what Joe expected heaven to be. As they are completing the tour Joe sees the warehouse building and again asks Peter to show it to him. Peter says no, it would make you unhappy. Joe made a break for the open warehouse door. Peter makes no attempt to stop him. Once inside, Joe sees row upon row of shelving stacked with white boxes each with a red ribbon around it. Joe notices that each box has a name on it. He asks Peter if there would be one with his own name on it. Peter says yes, but you don't want to see it because it would just make you sad. Joe noticed that the names were in alphabetical order so he raced down the rows of shelving. With a name like Smith it took him a long time to find the package, but when he did, he opened it, his countenance fell, because inside was a list of all the things that God wanted to give Joe while he was alive on earth, but Joe had never asked for them—so he never received them. Ask and you will receive.

Now the next example of the value of asking is for the guys who are reading this. Remember when you were in high school? There was this gal who you thought was really pretty neat. She was always very popular, and you thought you would like to ask her for a date, but you never did. You just knew that she would say no, and you didn't want that rejection. So you never asked her.

Now it's your twenty-year class reunion. You're in the meeting room where the reunion is being held. You're talking to one of your old classmates. You look up and see that girl that you thought was so neat. She sees you and immediately makes a bee line for you. She says, you know when we were in school, I really had a crush on you! And you never knew because you never asked! Well, don't worry about it now because it probably turned out better for you anyway.

Someone said, "all other things being equal, the mere act of asking can be the main difference between one person's success and another person's mediocre station in life. If you have nothing to lose by asking, by all means ASK." How many opportunities have we lost because we didn't ask, for whatever reason? Many times we are afraid to ask, but what do we have to lose?

Years ago a lady came to call on my business about phone service. She came from Denver, Colorado. She said, "no one can say no unless you ask." If they say no, I ask why not? If they say you need this or that skill, I acquire it. Now, that is a positive attitude! She knew she was not going to achieve unless she hung in there with the right questions and the right answers.

Fairly recently I talked to a development person from an organization with which I was familiar. I told him that when he went to the home area of a friend of mine that he should stop and see this friend. I said that he had plenty of money and was a good prospect for a gift to the organization. I talked to my friend later after this person had been to his house, and asked how it had come out. My friend said that this person had spent some four hours at his house. I said, "well what did you give?" He said, "well, he never asked so I never gave." All it would have taken was the ASK! The good news is that my friend did give when asked at a later date.

This poem pretty much sums up the value of asking. The author is Jesse Ritttenhouse, and it goes something like this:

**I bargained with life for a penny and life would pay no more,
however I begged in the evening as I counted scanty score.
Now life is a just employer, it pays you what you ask,
but once you've set your wages, now you must bear the task.
I worked for a menials hire, only to learn dismayed,
that any wage I'd ASKED of life, life would have surely paid.**

If we're going to be "water walkers" we've got to get out of the boat. We've got to get out of our comfort zones. We've got to be bold!

BELIEVE We've asked for it, now we have to believe that we can accomplish it. When we can see in our mind's eye what we want to do or be, and we truly believe it, then we will see it happen in our own lives.

Jesus said in Mark 11:4, "I say to you, whatever things you ask when you pray, believe that you receive them, and you will have them." Notice that He uses the present tense when He says "believe that you receive them." It's like we have to mentally believe that what we asked for has already materialized.

One thing that helps us believe is to affirm that we already have what we asked for. If we have asked for confidence, we affirm in the present tense; I am confident. I make the right decision. I do the right thing. Never say I will. Say I am.

COMMIT Someone in Waco, Texas, years ago, said that a good definition of commitment is that "commitment means that you don't have to decide." Stop and think about that. Let it sink in. "Commitment means that you don't

have to decide." For instance, you're in college; you've committed to get a 4.0 grade point average. You're well on your way to accomplishing that. You know that you can do it if you do well on the final test and if you really study. Someone suggests that your group should take the weekend off to party. Sure you would like to do it, and maybe you could still get a decent grade. You're committed to a 4.0 so the decision has already been made.
Commitment means you don't have to decide. You made that decision when you committed!

DO If we want to walk on water, we have to get out of the boat. If we're going to achieve anything significant, we're going to have to do things we've never done before. We're going to have to get out of our comfort zones and not be intimidated by the "wind and waves." We can have all kinds of good ideas and intentions but ultimately we have to make it happen. We have to just do it!

EXPECT We have to expect success in whatever we undertake. To get the most out of life we have to expect a lot. Really, what we're talking about is a positive mental attitude. A positive attitude expects the best. We know we will succeed in anything we attempt. Even when bad things happen to us we expect to benefit from the set back. We have to expect success in everything we do.

FOCUS Do you remember the signs that were beside the highways years ago? The kind that had something like a series of four signs spaced out every 600 feet or so. One went like this:

Little boy
with cheeks of tan
where were you
when it hit the fan?

Now that's not my message, but you can get the cadence that you get as you drive along and read the signs. The message is **successful people are the few who focus in and follow through**.

If we're to be successful in any area, we have to really focus in to make sure we know what we need to do. If we are delegating the implementation of a project, we have to make sure that the implementer understands the focus. We then need to follow up to make sure it's getting done. Someone said that which is monitored or followed up on gets done. Successful people are the few who focus in and follow through.

If we are to be "water walkers" we need to ask, believe, commit, do, expect, and focus.

NOTES

CHAPTER 33

The Most Important Person In The World

Who is the most important living person in the world? Think about that for a moment. Who would you pick? No matter who you picked, you're right! The reason you are right is that this person is a customer. To a business, the customer is the most important person. Without the customer the whole economy grinds to a standstill.

With that in mind, how do we take care of the customer? How do we keep him or her coming to us? Someone may say, I don't have to deal with customers, but ultimately we all do. Regardless of your job, a customer has to be served. Maybe your job is a few steps removed from the customer, and you may have support staff to serve the customer. Your support staff may be your immediate customer. How you treat the support staff (your customers) will be reflected by how the customers are treated by you. There is no business that can survive without the customer.

With that as a background, let's concentrate on meeting the customer face to face.

What does the customer look at?
1. **They look at the equipment, the facilities, and the appearance of the personnel.**
2. **They look at the ability of the personnel to provide the services offered.**
3. **They look at how they're treated and the promptness with which they are handled.**

I feel that the most important business issue is how we relate to the customer. I have said many times that in my business, I would rather have an average mechanic who relates well to people than a better mechanic without the people skills.

Jan Carlzon, C.E.O. of Scandinavian Airlines (SAS), took over the ailing airline in 1981. A year later he had taken the airline from losses to substantial profits. This was accomplished through customer service, giving the employees at every level the opportunity to make their own decisions at the Moments of Truth. Mr. Carlzon describes a Moments of Truth as a customer contact. Each customer contact is a critical opportunity to win or lose business based on how the company is perceived.

Mr. Carlzon, in his book *Moments of Truth*, writes, "last year each of our 10,000,000 passengers came in contact with approximately five SAS employees and this contact lasted an average of fifteen seconds at a time. Thus SAS is created in the minds of our customers 50,000,000 times a year, 15 seconds at a time. These 50,000,000 moments of truth are the moments that ultimately will determine whether SAS will succeed or fail as a company. They are the moments when we must prove to our customers that SAS is their best alternative."

What we need to do is to look at our businesses through our customers' eyes. If you were a customer at your business, how would you want to be treated? What would it take to create favorable moments of truth? We would do well to stop right here and have each one make a list of how we would like to be treated in our business, and then ask our selves, is it happening? Every time?

I was asked to make such a list at a college customer service class several years ago. My list would go something like this as it applies to our service and repair business at our gasoline service stations.

I would want to be:

- **Greeted warmly.**
- **Waited on promptly. (Have you ever pulled up to a service bay at a service station and no one pays any attention to you?)**
- **I would want someone to listen (really listen) to me about my cars problems.**

- They would thoroughly analyze my problem.
- The work would be done well (and they would explain what they did).
- The work would be done on time.
- I would be charged fairly.
- I would feel appreciated.
- I would be treated friendly, attentively, courteously, and enthusiastically.
- And it would happen every time!

Let's make the most of our MOMENTS OF TRUTH!

Here are some key customer service facts:

- A satisfied customer will tell 4–5 people.
- A dissatisfied customer will tell 8–10 people
- Approximately one in four business customers have complaints. An average business never hears about ninety-six percent of these problems. Sounds high doesn't it?
- Over ninety-five percent of these complaints can be handled satisfactorily. These customers will tell an average of five people. (Positively!)
- The biggest reason customers have complaints is because of poor or indifferent treatment received from sales or service people.
- It takes twelve positive actions to make up for a negative experience a customer receives. With all these customer facts in mind, it makes sense to treat the customers right and do the job right the first time!

Let's take care of the most important person in the world, THE CUSTOMER!

CHAPTER 34

Who Is Our Customer? What Does Our Customer Really Want?

We have at least two kinds of customers. First, we have the customer to whom we are trying to sell our product or service. Second, we have for customers the people that we are working with and need their cooperation to successfully complete the transaction with the ultimate customer. In other words we cannot successfully, consistently serve our ultimate customer unless we have the wholehearted cooperation of our fellow workers, who should have the same goals as we do. Unless we can successfully take care of our ultimate customer, we are soon out of business. It takes the cooperation of everyone in the business (the internal customers) to sell the external customers our goods.

We must always remember that it takes a team to accomplish the complete sales task. If we don't treat our internal customers (our fellow workers) with respect, we make our job of serving the ultimate customer very difficult or impossible.

Then we get to the part of the sales transaction where we say do we really know (or really care) what the customer wants. If we don't, we are never going to be really successful. Sometimes we are so concerned with what's in it for us that we forget what the customer really needs or wants.

An acquaintance was standing around a hamburger shack in a border town, eating a hamburger. He heard the phone in the shack ring and immediately the owner started grilling several hamburgers and put on some French fries. He completed the order and yelled out, "Jose!" Immediately a young Mexican boy, probably no more than ten years old, appeared from behind the shack. He picked up the sack and took off on the run to deliver the food to a business place some blocks away.

The acquaintance continued eating his burger and watched what was going to happen. Soon Jose came back on a dead run. He had delivered the goods. The man who had been watching wanted to talk to the young boy. He said to Jose, "you ran all the way to deliver the food and now you run back empty handed just as fast. Why?" Jose responded. "My customers want hot fries; I deliver hot fries!" He wanted to make sure that he got back in time so that other customers would also get hot fries.

Let's determine what our customers (internal and external) really want (including great service), and give it to them EVERY TIME.

I would like to extend the customer service to go beyond our business relationships.

Let's include our everyday relationships with the people with whom we come into contact every day. Let's include our friends, too. How about our spouses?

OUR MISSION

Every business should know what its mission in business is.
What is our mission? How are we going to accomplish it?

Our mission in our business is:

To make our businesses customer-driven.
To provide outstanding service to our customers.
To do more for the customer than they can reasonably expect.
To do a thorough job on the customers' cars so that we can sell them what they need. We are the experts. Our customers expect us to tell them what they need. We owe that to the customer.
To perform the kind of job that we can be proud of.
To be profitable!

QUALITY CUSTOMER SERVICE

Always answer the phone immediately. Answer with the business name, the employee name, and then, "how may I help you?"

PRIORITIES

1. SELL SOMETHING
2. CLEAN SOMETHING
3. LEARN SOMETHING

There is never a time when there is nothing to do!

MORE PRIORITIES

The customer always comes first!

A. The customer at the cash register is "more first" than the customer waiting to have a tire repaired or a car to be fixed. The point is that someone cannot be kept waiting for something that can be handled quickly.

B. If you are cleaning, inventorying, or whatever, the customer must be served promptly.

C. A person being given directions when a customer comes to the cash register is told "excuse me, I'll be right back with you." The customer is always the priority.

JOB DESCRIPTIONS

I believe that our employees will do a better job for our customers if they understand what their job or position really is and what the expectations are. The following is the job description for the cashiers at our gasoline service stations.

1. To make each customer feel welcome and appreciated.
2. To show customers that we're concerned about them immediately, to greet and ask them if we can help them.
3. To provide outstanding service in all our dealings with the customer.
   A. Greet customers warmly.
   B. Ask if they need anything more (snacks and so forth). That's a service, but you also sell more if you ask!
   C. Collect (now that's important!).
   D. Thank them warmly when you complete the transaction— and, of course, ask them to come back!
4. Keep store neat and well stocked.
5. When not busy with other things, keep the station clean. Let's have customers comment on how neat we are.
6. Help wherever and whenever it's needed–don't wait to be asked.
7. Take care of customer problems or complaints immediately if possible. Most problems can be taken care of by listening and trying to help.
8. Treat people like they are important. They are!
9. Dress and groom neatly and cleanly and in approved uniform.
10. Do more for customers than they can reasonably expect. Go the extra mile.

CROWING CUSTOMER

MISSION STATEMENT

To develop knowledgeable, excited, and enthusiastic employees, who in turn create crowing customers. My definition of Crowing Customers: to have our customers so happy with our service that they don't keep it a secret. They "crow" to their friends. They tell their friends how happy they are with us. They recommend us to their friends.

HOW TO MAKE CROWING CUSTOMERS

1. Call people by name.
2. Smile!
3. Always answer the phone with the service station name. Then say, "Jerry speaking, how may I help you?"
4. Bathrooms super nice and clean.
5. Grooming and cleanliness of drive and grounds, including clean pumps, rubbish can, squeegees, and washer solvent.
6. Employees have clean uniforms and name tags.
7. Pay attention to the customer immediately.
8. Knowledgeable employees.
9. Well trained employees.
10. Back room (shop)
    A. Cars vacuumed every time.
    B. Every car checked out and inspected with a checklist.
    C. Mechanics explain to the customer what they will do or what they did to the car.
11. The whole building clean.
12. All of these items and services done every time and every time and every time and every time!

CHAPTER 35

Making Positive Deposits In Other People's Lives

O ne of my habits on Sunday mornings was to exercise on my exercycle while watching, first of all, the Crystal Cathedral Church service from Garden Grove, California, from 7 AM to 8 AM. After that I would listen to Joel Osteen's church service from Houston, Texas, for another half hour. After that I go to our regular church, Lord of Life Lutheran, in Maple Grove, Minnesota.

One Sunday morning Joel Osteen's sermon had to do with making positive deposits in other people's lives and avoiding making withdrawals. My prayer for a period of time was for me to go out of my way to build people up, to help make them feel good about themselves. This was important to me because sometimes in jest I have a tendency to cut people down, and I would hate for anyone to take it seriously. I am just having fun, but I would hate for anyone to take it the wrong way.

So, my prayer was that I would have a chance to make people feel good about themselves. I want to compliment as many people as I can and to be specific. General compliments can seem rather bland and insincere. I want to be honest and specific. I want to show care and concern for others. I want to be alert to the needs of others.

Imagine the difference that we could make in our work place and in our community if each of us would concentrate on building others up.

CHAPTER 36

Acting "As If"

S o you go to work in the morning, and you do not feel very motivated. You're kind of down. You don't feel very happy. Nothing seems quite right. What do you do? Do you just mope around and pass on your contagious disease to all of the other employees? Now you have all kinds of people depressed.

In orientation meetings that I had with new employees, I would tell them that if they come to work and were in a bad mood for whatever reason, that that was not the customers' problem. I told them not to pass that bad mood or attitude on to the customer. I told them to act as if they were happy, and soon they would be happy and they wouldn't know which came first. Were they already happy or were they happy because the acted as if they were happy? Which came first, the act or the happiness? Who really cares as long as it works? William James said, "you do not sing because you are happy, you are happy because you sing."

We can use the acting as if principle in many areas of our lives. If we're afraid, we can act as if we're brave. If we're tired, we act as if we are refreshed. We are in control of our lives. If we are somewhat shy and have difficulty interacting with other people we don't know, we can take charge by acting as if we are really anxious to meet other people and that people really like us. Two things will happen. We will enjoy those people whose friendship we are growing and the second thing is that they will like us.

Let's not let other people or circumstances control how we feel about something. We can control our thoughts, and our thoughts control us. Many of our likes and dislikes are really unfounded and based on either bad information or no information. Maybe we don't like certain foods, but we have never tried them. The list of things that we're "not good at" or with which we're "not comfortable" could go on and on.

If we're not happy with where we're at, we need to make some changes. We need to act as if we are enjoying the changes and we will. You may say that this just isn't me, I don't have the confidence. Wait a second, that is what it's all about. If you're not confident, act as if you're confident! If we are willing to spend some effort on ourselves, we can become the people we want to be.

So what are we saying? We're saying that we have a choice. We make the choice of who we want to be and what we want to do. We have a choice in all the things we do in life. We can choose to be the way we've always been or we can choose the way we've always wanted to be and we can make the necessary changes. We make the change and we change our lives.

NOTES

CHAPTER 37

Grandpa Days

I t must be about nine years ago that my three grandchildren were competing so much for my attention when they came over to our house that I decided I needed a plan if I was going to keep them happy. If my time period of nine years is right, then Sami my granddaughter would have been five years old and my two grandsons Andy and Dane would have been seven years old (not twins, different families). Sami and Andy are the children of my son Dean and his wife, Pam. Dane is the son of my older son, Jay. Both of our sons live very close to us in Maple Grove, Minnesota, which Mary and I think is wonderful.

My plan was to have Grandpa Days where I would have one grandchild for a whole day and then keep that going on a rotating basis with each one of them. It developed into a system where the grandchild would decide what we would do for the day that he or she would be with me. This Grandpa Day has turned into a highlight for me. It gives me a chance to really get to know what each one of them is thinking and a chance to talk about it.

When Sami was five or six years, we were on a Grandpa Day, in downtown Minneapolis by the Mississippi River. We had seen the locks that the boats go through and had walked across the historic Stone Arch Bridge. As we were walking along, Sami said to me, "Grandpa, tell me a story—and make it fiction." I said OK. When I was five years old, I was a rough, tough cowboy. (Actually, when I was five years old, I kind of thought I was a cowboy.) I was walking along out in the country, and I ran across some rough, tough cowboys who were trying to bust this bronco so they could ride it. Now this was a really mean horse. All of the cowboys tried to ride it. None of them could ride the horse. He was such a mean horse, so they decided they would just give up.

I looked at that horse. I walked up to him and looked him in the eye. I reached into my pocket and took out a sugar cube. I held out my hand with the sugar cube in it. The horse ate the sugar cube right out of my hand. I looked that horse in the eyes, and I could see that the horse wanted me to ride him, so I hopped onto the horse, and I had no problem at all riding him. At this point, I thought my story was over but Sami said, "Grandpa, there's a lesson in that!" I said Sami, "What's the lesson?" She said, "You just can't force somebody to do something that they don't want to do." So, what she was really saying is that if you want to get somebody to do something that they don't want to do, there has to be something in it for them.

When Andy was 7 years old, we were on a Grandpa Day, and we were again walking downtown by the Mississippi River. Out of the blue, Andy asked me if I had any stock. I told him yes, that I have some stock, but not a lot because our money was in the businesses and in buildings. He said, "Do you have any one stock that is about half of all the stock you own?" I said yes. He said, "Is it better to have a lot of one stock or is it better to have a lot of different shares of stock?" I said it is better to have a lot of different shares of stock. Andy said, "Do you have any mutual funds? I said yes, I have some mutual funds. He said something like, "are mutual funds better?" I said that mutual funds bought and sold within the fund could cause some income taxes that would be out of your control. Andy said, "If you say that it is better to have a lot of different stocks, shouldn't you know what stocks your mutual fund is buying so that you are not buying the same thing?" I guess you can't argue with that.

It really amazed me that he understood the stock market well enough to ask these intelligent and insightful questions. I asked him if he had been talking to his dad about these things and he said no. I don't know where he came up with his questions, but I was impressed.

Dane, on his Grandpa Days with me, has a wide variety of things he wants to do. At about age twelve, he started wanting to include time to go around to car dealerships to look at cars. He is so interested in cars. He looked a little old for his age so the car sales people were willing to spend time talking about cars, and of course we would have to tell them they would have to wait awhile.

Dane is very interested in music and now is involved in a small group in which he is on the drums. He is constantly looking on Grandpa Days for me to get him something new for his music interests. That's another part of Grandpa Days—they have a budget on what they can buy for themselves, and sometimes the budget is exceeded. But that's part of being a Grandpa.

When Sami was around seven years old, I was doing a Grandpa Day with her, and I didn't tell her what was in store for her that day. First of all just to give you a little background, I was scheduled for about one hour at mid-day on this Saturday to do some make-up training for some Rotary Club presidents-elect. They had been scheduled for training that we do in Evanston, Illinois, which is the international headquarters of Rotary International, but they were unable to be there at the main training session.

At this meeting there are 15–20 presidents-elect present. Sami and I come in and sit in the back of the room. The meeting is in progress. I whisper to Sami that when they introduce me that she is to go right up to the front of the room with me. (Up to this point she had no clue as to what was happening). I was now introduced, and Sami didn't hesitate at all. I introduced Sami and told a couple of stories about her that related to the training.

We were then into the main part of the talk, and I said that when presidents are selecting key people to do the real important positions in your club, don't just ask a body, make sure that it is someone who will really do a good job. As I was talking, some one directed my attention to Sami who had her hand up. I acknowledged Sami and she said, "If you have a problem like that, what do you do about it, and how do you correct it?" She had one other point in the program where she asked another question.

We are done and the MC comes up to shake our hand. The incoming Rotary district governor comes to us to escort us out, and Sami reaches out to shake his hand. We get outside to go to the parking lot and Sami says, "I WAS THE STAR."

Grandpa Days still go on. As I am finishing the book, Sami is fourteen, Andy is seventeen, and Dane is seventeen. Within the last month, each of them has been on a Grandpa Day with me. There has been some fun and some shopping.

CHAPTER 38

Ethical Will

T his year we had a speaker at our Roseville Rotary Club. The subject of his talk was ethical wills, which I had never heard of. As he was talking about it, I thought that it was something that I could use at the end of the book that I was writing. Matter of fact, this is the book!

What is an ethical will? An ethical will is really ideas, thoughts, and emotions that you would want to pass on to the next generations in your family. This would be expressions of love, of caring, and of advising and admonishing. The time to do this as far as I am concerned is now. I would like to pass on some feelings, guidance, and perhaps some advice. Also, I would like to show that I care about what happens to you after I've left the face of this earth.

I know that advice is not always looked for, and not always welcome, and probably not always as valuable as I might think. I am writing this book as a motivational book with some biographical content. One of my purposes is that I want to pass on to my children and grandchildren some thoughts that are important to me, and probably one might not have a chance to sit down with those closest to you and discuss cares, concerns, and opportunities. I do not want to wait till the last moment to pass along some thoughts. I decided I wanted to include those in my ethical will at the end of the book. I want my children, grand children, and maybe my great-grandchildren to think about where I'm coming from before I meet my maker.

With that in mind, I want to say to my wife, Mary, that I love you with all my heart and that every year gets better and better. I thank God for you and hope that we have lots more years to have fun together. It's been a great 50 years together at this point, so now we can start working on the next 50!

To Jay, my older son, I want you to know that I love you immensely and appreciate your humor and personality. I always enjoy being a guest in your house. You're not only a good son, you know how to cook and entertain. Mom and I are so glad that Wendy has become a part of our family this year. Wendy adds a lot. This year of 2006 with you and Wendy getting married has been special. I love you, Wendy.

To Dean, my younger son, I want to say I love you greatly. I think you know that in our businesses over the years, you have made my life easy because of your knowledge and skills, and that you have kept up with all the technology. You have always been there when I needed you— and you don't even complain about it! You seem to anticipate the needs. Dean, you know how to pick a wife. Mom and I are happy that you chose Pam. I love you, Pam. We could not have asked for a better daughter-in-law than you. You did everything to make your wedding special—except for that extremely hot weather. We enjoyed surprising you when you turned around from the ceremony to all of the pink Happy Hankies the whole crowd was waving.

Now I want to talk a little about my grandchildren from the oldest to the youngest.

Dane, I love you a whole bunch. I enjoy your sense of humor and all your musical ability. You are definitely good company.

Andy, I love you so much. You are always there when I need you. I don't know what I would do without all your computer skills. It's a good thing you're only two blocks away. Someday when I grow up, I want to be as smart as you!

Sami, you are my favorite granddaughter. The first time I told you that, you said, "not to mention, I'm your only granddaughter." Sami, at fourteen, you are not only a hockey player, but you are a very pretty lady. You absolutely sparkle! I love you oodles.

I hope all three of you, my grandchildren, never get too tired of me telling you how much I love you. Always remember the way you have been brought up, that you are Christians. There are many temptations to maybe do something that you shouldn't do. I pray that Jesus will always be with you and guide you.

Always tell the truth—then you will never need a great memory to cover your tracks.

I know that sometimes you thought that I spent too much time on Rotary International stuff, but remember this Rotary four-way test of all we think, do, or say.

Ask yourself: Is it the truth? Is it fair to all concerned? Will it build goodwill and better friendships? Will it be beneficial to all concerned? If we pass the test with these questions all being answered yes, we're on the right track. Treat people the way you want to be treated all the time.

Always remember that we are put in this world to make it a better place. Always try to understand where someone else is coming from mentally, and why they think the way they do. Treat other people the way you want to be treated.

Be empathetic—when someone says something that might have a tendency to irritate you—don't let it. Realize that this person may be going through some tough times in their life and they need understanding, not criticism. If you want to have friends, be a friend.

When someone does or says something to you that hurts you in some way, never hold a grudge. Forgive and forget. Life is too short not to forgive. If you hold a grudge, it really hurts no one but you. Let go, really let go.

Always have a positive, can-do attitude. If you believe you can, you can do about anything you want to do. Look for the best in other people. Build other people up. Be sure to compliment others for doing something well, or at least for trying to do something well. Always try to make others feel good about them-selves.

Don't be afraid to make mistakes. Don't feel any less successful when something doesn't turn out the way you want it to. This is all a part of the learning process. Don't give up.

Feel good about yourself anyway or any time.

Always be a giver. Jesus said, "Give, and it will be given unto you, good measure, pressed down and running over will be put into your lap, for the measure that you use to give will be the measure you get back." Giving is an important part of living. Generosity is an important virtue in life.

Live life to the fullest, and make the most of it. I will be cheering for all of you, all the time. I will enjoy my time with you, and I will be enjoying seeing you be successful in all that you do.

Bibliography

In writing this book, every attempt was made to seek out the original sources used. Unfortunately, some information could not be located, and I apologize to the original authors who are not cited here.
—Jerry Showalter

Brott, Rich, and Frank Damazio. *Biblical Principles for Releasing Financial Provision!* Washington: ABC Book Publishing, 2005.

Baines, Barney K. *Ethical Wills*. New York: De Capo Press, 2002.

Canfield, Jack L., and Janet Switzer. *The Success Principles™: How to Get from Where You Are to Where You Want to Be*. New York: HarperCollins, 2005.

Carnegie, Dale. *How to Win Friends & Influence People*. New York: Pocket, 1998.

Carothers, Merlin. *Power in Praise*. Escondido, CA: Merlin R. Carothers, 1980.

Carlzon, Jan. *Moments of Truth*. New York: Harper & Row, 1989.

Covey, Stephen R. *The 7 Habits of Highly Effective People: Powerful Lessons in Personal Change*. New York: Free Press, 1990.

Dobkins, Carl, Jr. "My Heart Is an Open Book." Lyrics Download. http://www.lyricsdownload.com/carl-dobkins-jr-my-heart-is-an-open-book-lyrics.html.

Felipe. "Niagara Falls." *Habitat for Humanity Newsletter*, April 2006.

Hurston, Joe, and Martha Van Cise. *Run to the Roar*. Lake Mary, FL: Charisma House, 2006.

Meyer, Paul J. *Unlocking Your Legacy: 25 Keys for Success*. New York: Moody, 2003.

Ortberg, John. *If You Want to Walk on Water, You'd Better Get Out of the Boat*. Grand Rapids, MI: Zondervan, 2001.

Penney, J. C. *Fifty Years with the Golden Rule (A Spiritual Autobiography)*. New York: Harper & Brothers, 1950.

Robinson, Jonathan. *Real Wealth: A Spiritual Approach to Money and Work*. Carlsbad, CA: Hay House, Inc., 1998.

Schuller, Robert. *Don't Throw Away Tomorrow—Crystal Cathedral Edition*. New York: HarperOne, 2005.

"*SMART.*" http://en.wikipedia

UCSB Exercise & Sport Studies Recreation. "Attitudes Are Everything." University of California, Santa Barbara. http://www.essr.ucsb.edu/recsports/handouts/0206/attitudesareeverything.pdf.

Ziglar, Zig. *See You at the Top: 25th Anniversary Edition*. Gretna, LA: Pelican Publishing, 2000.

_____. *Steps to the Top (Motivational Series)*. Gretna, LA: Pelican Publishing, 1985.

NOTES

NOTES

NOTES